Greek Mythology

Your All-Access Guide to the Gods, Heroes, and Monsters of Ancient Greece | Discover the Most Captivating Characters of Ancient Greece Myth

Steven Latmers

Table of Contents

Chapter 1: Introduction to Greek Mythology 5

What is Greek Mythology? 5

Overview of Ancient Greek Civilization 7

Religion and the Role of Myths in Ancient Greece..................... 11

Primary Sources for the Myths.. 15

Chapter 2: The Gods and Goddesses.................................... 20

Cosmogony: Origins of the Universe................................ 20

The Titans 22

The Olympians: Main Greek Gods and Goddesses 29

Other Deities 34

Chapter 3: Heroes and Demigods 37

The Concept of Heroism in Ancient Greece 37

Famous Greek Heroes (Heracles, Perseus, Theseus etc.)............. 40

Demigods and Other Mortals Who Became Legends 44

Chapter 4: Significant Myths and Legends 47

Myths of Creation and the Cosmos 47

Myths About the Olympian Gods 50

The Trojan War and Homer's Epics 55

Myths of Adventure and Heroism 57

Tragic Myths of Love and Betrayal 61

Chapter 5: Mythical Creatures and Monsters 64

Creatures of the Sea and Waterways 64

Dangerous Creatures and Killers 66

Mythical Animals 70

Hybrids and Monsters... 73

Chapter 6: The Underworld and Afterlife.............................. 78

The Realm of Hades... 78

The Rivers and Regions of the Greek Underworld................... 80

The Dead, Punishments, and the Judgment of Souls 84

Chapter 7: Archaeological Sites and Artifacts 89

Temples, Sanctuaries, and Other Sacred Sites..........................89

Treasures and Artifacts Found at Key Locations 91

Ancient Texts and Manuscripts Related to the Myths.................95

Chapter 8: The Legacy and Influence of Greek Myths 98

Myths in Later Greek and Roman Times 98

Representations in Art and Literature Over the Centuries..........101

Myths That Continue to Inspire Our Culture Today 105

Chapter 1: Introduction to Greek Mythology

What is Greek Mythology?

Mythology had an essential role in both the religious and secular practices of ancient Greece. Mythological tales not only helped to explain occurrences in the natural world, but also supplied important life lessons that contributed to the formation of civilization. Through its everlasting narrative and intriguing cast of gods, heroes, and mythological monsters, Greek mythology continues to grab our imaginations today.

The myths of ancient Greece originated as oral traditions and were afterwards written down in literary works such as Homer's Iliad and Odyssey. The environment of ancient Greek polytheism, which considered deities as integral to every part of life, was conducive to the development and flourishing of mythology. The fact that gods and goddesses had human emotions like jealously, rage, and passion made their exploits more exciting and sympathetic to the audience. stories provided explanations for phenomena that were otherwise unexplained, such as the creation of the world, weather patterns, and the changing of the seasons. These stories gave meaning to experiences that would have been meaningless without them.

The mythology of ancient Greece centered on a group of gods known as the Olympians, who were said to reign from a mountain called Olympus. Hera, Zeus' sister and wife, stood by his side while he ruled supremely as king of the gods during their time together. Other important Olympians include Poseidon, the god of the sea, Demeter, the goddess of harvest and fertility, Ares, the crafty warrior, and Apollo and Artemis, the twins, who are linked with the sun, the moon, and hunting. Each god was responsible for a certain area of life, like as love, battle, or the underworld. Their fights and love affairs became legendary tales that continue to hold the attention of spectators in the contemporary era.

Mortal heroes like as Heracles, Theseus, and Odysseus carried out heroic exploits and embarked on expeditions that contributed to the development of early Greek civilization while the gods on Olympus fought and plotted. Other legendary beings include the chimera, who could breathe fire, and the Minotaur, who was half-human and half-bull.

The Garden of the Hesperides, which was said to be located in a remote part of the world and was protected by a dragon, was one of the spectacular locations that was described in mythical travel accounts.

Greek mythology continues to have a significant impact on western culture to this day, from its legacy in contemporary film series such as "Percy Jackson" and "Clash of the Titans" to the ways in which it has shaped philosophy, architecture, and the arts. The examination of universally applicable human experiences contained in Greek myths assures that they will remain a source of motivation for many generations to come, regardless of whether these stories are read for pleasure or as meaningful cultural narratives.

Themes and Tales Derived from Mythology

Mythology didn't just focus on explaining the gods; it also probed significant ideas about human nature and ethical behavior. Stories about hubris instilled a sense of humility in people, such as the one about Icarus flying dangerously near to the sun. The story of Orpheus and Eurydice is often cited as an example of profound love and heartbreaking betrayal.

Events such as the Trojan War were retold in well-known cycles found in mythology. The Iliad included a description of Achilles' fury as well as the decisive moments of the fight. The Odyssey recounts the story of Odysseus' ten-year voyage home, during which he fought monsters along the route like the Cyclops.

The Foundations of the Myths

Although oral traditions were the source of myths' beginnings, subsequent written works served to reinforce their tales. Epics and thiogenic poetry that are considered to be foundational were written by Homer, Hesiod, and other poets. Through their dramatic performances, tragedians like as Aeschylus, Sophocles, and Euripides helped solidify myths.
There was also a continuation of mythology in visual art. The ceramics at the temple reflected popular tales, while the sculptures in the temple showed gods and legendary situations. Mosaics discovered at archaeological sites served as a textless medium for the transmission of tales.

Various Perspectives on the Various Tales

Myths have been understood by scholars to be allegories having deeper and more significant symbolic meanings. The deeds of the gods were used to illustrate the cosmic orders and forces that existed before the universe. The place of mankind in the world was better understood thanks to myths.

Overview of Ancient Greek Civilization

The Ancient Greek civilization is a cornerstone upon which a significant portion of Western art, culture, politics, and philosophy were established. This civilization expanded over the Mediterranean over the course of more than a thousand years, from the Bronze Age to the Roman conquest in the second century BC. Along the way, it left an unmistakable mark that may still be felt even in our times.

The time period is often separated into many eras, including the Bronze Age (which occurred around 3000–1200 BC), the Dark Ages (which occurred around 1200-800 BC), the Archaic Age (which occurred around 800-500 BC), the Classical Age (which occurred around 500-323 BC), and the Hellenistic Age (which occurred around 323–30 BC).

During the time period known as the Bronze Age, three important civilizations emerged: the Cycladic, the Minoan on the island of Crete, and the Mycenaean on the mainland of Greece. In particular, the Mycenaeans were famous for their military-oriented culture, their fortified palaces, and their adoption of the Linear B script. The stories that occurred during this time period, like as the Siege of Troy, would eventually provide as motivation for Homer to write his epic poetry.

The demise of the Mycenaean civilization, for reasons that aren't entirely clear, ushered in a time in Greek history known as the Dark Ages. Due to the fact that there are no written documents from this time period, very little information is known about it. On the other hand, it is generally accepted that this was a period of time when both population and mobility were on the decline.

After emerging from the Dark Ages, Greece entered the Archaic Age, which was a time of recovery and development during which the country flourished. The spread of Greek culture throughout the

Mediterranean was a direct effect of Greek colonization. The Phoenician script gave way to the Greek alphabet, which was eventually adopted, and the polis, often known as a city-state, emerged as the dominant form of political organization.

Athens and Sparta, the two most powerful city-states in Greece at the time, rose to prominence during the Classical Age, which is also known as the Golden Age of Greece. Athens was the birthplace of democracy, whereas Sparta evolved into a civilization based on military might. During this time period, great progress was made in a variety of fields, including science, philosophy, architecture, and sculpture. During this time period, some of the greatest minds in history and philosophy, including Socrates, Plato, and Aristotle, as well as some of the greatest tragedians, such Aeschylus, Sophocles, and Euripides, and historians, like Herodotus and Thucydides, came into being. The Persian Wars and the subsequent expansion of the Athenian maritime empire occurred during this time period, and they were followed by the catastrophic Peloponnesian War, which was fought between Athens and Sparta.

The beginning of the Hellenistic Age may be pinpointed to the year 323 BC, when Alexander the Great passed away. Because of Alexander the Great's conquests, Greek culture was able to disseminate far and wide throughout this time period, even making its way to India. During the Hellenistic Age, improvements were made in a variety of subjects, like as mathematics and astronomy. Additionally, the well-known Library of Alexandria was founded during this time period. This period lasted from the beginning of the Hellenistic era to the Roman invasion of Greece in 30 BC.

The ancient Greeks adhered to a polytheistic religious philosophy, which centered their devotion on a pantheon of gods and goddesses, each of whom was associated with a particular sphere of influence. The performance of rituals, the offering of sacrifices, and the celebration of religious holidays were important components of religious life, and the telling of myths was essential to the process of explaining natural occurrences, human qualities, and religious activities.

Grains, grapes, and olives were the principal agricultural products that contributed to Ancient Greece's economy, which was predominately dependent on agriculture. The importance of commerce cannot be overstated, particularly given the role that the Mediterranean Sea and the Aegean Sea played as bustling commercial networks. Slavery was an institution that was strongly ingrained, and a significant number of households were owners of slaves who worked in a variety of roles. Greek society was split between free citizens and slaves, with further distinctions made between males and women in terms of their standing as citizens. While males were expected to take part in public life, including politics, women were often expected to stay at home and care for their families. On the other hand, this differed from city-state to city-state and changed throughout the course of history.

The legacy that Ancient Greece has left behind is incalculable. Its contributions to philosophic thought, political thought, literary thought, artistic thought, and scientific thought continue to have an impact on Western culture. This interesting and complicated culture is the cradle of such ideas as democracy, the logical approach to science, the ethics of philosophy, and the aesthetics of art. Learning about the ancient Greek civilization is not simply an exercise in historical research; it is also essential for getting a handle on a great deal of the contemporary world.

The ancient Greeks reached staggeringly high levels of accomplishment in a variety of artistic fields. The cultural production of Ancient Greece established standards that are still looked up to and respected to this day. These standards range from the architectural marvels of the Parthenon to the dramatic tragedies of Sophocles and the philosophical insights of Plato. Their artwork, whether it was in the shape of enormous sculptures or delicate ceramics, investigated the intricacies of the human experience. They captured moments of valor, desolation, love, and the divine in their works of art. Their oral storytelling culture, which was expressed in Homer's epic poems and the comedies, tragedies, and other plays that were performed in their theaters, was the foundation upon which Western literature was built. These works, which have stood the test of time, continue to motivate, test, and delight us while providing insights into the human experience that continue to be relevant even now.

The many social structures

In ancient Greece, the social structure was highly stratified, and each city-state had its own distinct social hierarchy. In general, people in society were classified as either free citizens (male or female), metrics (foreigners residing in Greece), or slaves. Free citizens included both men and women. Women, mesic people, and slaves had much less rights than free males had, including the inability to participate in government. Free men had the highest rights, including the capacity to vote.

Women in Ancient Greece often had less freedom than males had, particularly when compared to the same roles that men played in society. The principal obligations that fell on their shoulders were those of household management and child rearing. There were, however, a few notable outliers, the most notable of which was the city-state of Sparta, in which women were granted more freedoms as well as obligations.

In ancient Greece, the practice of slavery was well rooted and widespread. Slaves were utilized in many different capacities, ranging from general housework to highly specialized labor in professions like as education and the production of artisan goods. There is evidence that some slaves served in administrative capacities for the government.

Progress made in the field of philosophy

It is well knowledge that ancient Greece was the cradle of Western philosophical thought. The theoretical frameworks and methodological approaches to philosophy that were produced during this time period continue to be relevant now. The three most well-known philosophers to have lived during this time period are Socrates, Plato, and Aristotle.

The Socratic method is a kind of questioning that was developed by Socrates. Its purpose is to encourage critical thinking and to reveal the inconsistencies that exist in a participant's views. Plato, who had previously been instructed by Socrates, established the Academy in Athens and was Aristotle's teacher there. The teachings of Plato, a Greek philosopher, frequently concentrated on such concepts as justice, beauty, and equality. In addition to this, he penned works on a broad variety of subjects, such as political philosophy, religion, cosmology, epistemology, and the philosophy of language.

Aristotle, in his turn, made substantial contributions to a wide variety of subjects, including logic, metaphysics, mathematics, physics, biology, botany, ethics, politics, agriculture, medicine, dance, and theater. It is generally agreed that he was an important player in the development of Western philosophy and science.

The field of architecture

The architecture of ancient Greece is famous for being massive, symmetrical, and beautiful in appearance. Temples, theaters, and stadiums were frequently constructed on a colossal scale in Greek architecture, which is one of the characteristics that distinguishes Greek architecture from other architectural styles. Doric, Ionic, and Corinthian orders were the three types of columns that were utilized by the ancient Greeks. Each of these orders had their own unique proportions and decoration.

One of the most well-known and well-recognized examples of Greek architecture is the Parthenon, which was built as a temple to honor the goddess, Athena. It is a symbol of the cultural and political triumphs of Athens during its heyday and may be found in the city of the same name.

In conclusion, Ancient Greece was undeniably a society that accomplished a great deal during its history. Its vast and diversified contributions in the domains of philosophy, governance, art, and science have had a lasting influence on current society, which makes its study both intriguing and informative. These contributions have had an impact on everything from art to science to philosophy.

Religion and the Role of Myths in Ancient Greece

Religion and mythology in ancient Greece were intimately linked with one another. Not only were the gods and goddesses of the pantheon individuals that were described in tales, but they also served as the foundation for religious rites, celebrations, and everyday spiritual life. The ancient Greeks attempted to make sense of the world around them and win favor with their gods via the telling of tales.
The majority of city-states had formal state religions that were based on significant deities like as Zeus, Apollo, or Athena. Temples dedicated to these patron gods might be found at notable sites around the world. People would make sacrifices and worship before statues of gods in the hopes of receiving help with issues like as fertility, winning in combat, or finding a cure for disease. Oracles like as Delphi offered the prophecies that were requested from Apollo. Later on, there was also an emergence of mysterious faiths that involved performing hidden ceremonies.

Even if particular beliefs varied from place to place, the Greeks of all the numerous city-states usually adhered to the same pantheon. Not only did myths explain the origins of the gods and their connections with one another, but they also portrayed the gods as very human superbeings who intervened in the lives of mortals. For instance, Dionysus is credited with spreading the gift of wine across his religion; nonetheless, legends warned against inviting the god's insanity.

Gods were worshiped at civic rites and festivals by participating in processions, making sacrifices, dancing, and playing games. Pilgrims traveled to shrines in large Pan-Hellenic communities like as Delphi, Olympia, and Dodona because these places were the sites of legendary occurrences. Through the use of plays, drama evolved into a medium for retelling fundamental stories. Decorations and sayings that made reference to gods were two examples of how myths seeped into daily life.

Myths provided the Greeks with a common frame of reference through which they linked to one another and the universe, despite the fact that Greek religion departed from the more tight divides between myth and belief that are common today. They did this by providing explanations for natural occurrences and by bolstering ethical rules via the use of theatrical lectures. This interweaving of myth and religion was an essential component of ancient Greek society, which had a formative role in the development of Western civilization.

Even in today's modern architecture, literature, and art, mythological allusions continue to play a significant role. The stories continue to captivate the minds of readers by touching on timeless topics such as love, destiny, and the position of mankind in the wider universe. Their contribution helped ensure that Greek tales would remain popular for millennia to come.
The Part Played by Sacrifice

The ancient Greeks sought heavenly favor via the offering of sacrifices. They made sacrifices at both public and private altars by setting grain, fruit, animals, and libations on fire. In order to commemorate significant events like as battles and harvests, priests offered blood sacrifices. The most delicious portions were reserved for the gods, while the rest was distributed among the worshippers.

Oracles and clairvoyant predictions

In addition to Delphi, other oracles like as the grove of Dodona would also deliver prophesies. After experiencing trances, priests and priestesses would communicate the gods' enigmatic intentions to the people. Oracles were consulted by the Greeks before making significant choices about anything from marriage to war. As a result, oracular shrines were influential places.

Sacred Ministers: Priests and Priestesses

To take care of the shrines and act as representatives of the gods, each temple had clergy such as priests and priestesses. Sacrifices and ceremonies were presided over by priests. Priestesses like Pythia of Delphi were able to harness heavenly energy, yet they suffered from the social shame of being power brokers. Slaves at the temple were also used in religious activities.

Rituals Performed at Home and during Funerals

Religion was practiced in Greek households, and sacrifices were made to show reverence for gods and ancestor spirits. At funerals, sacrifices were offered and regulations governing burial customs were followed in order to pay respect to relatives who had passed on to Hades. Memorials served as an homage to the deceased through their journey into the afterlife.

Impact on the Study of Philosophy

Later thinkers discussed theology and interpreted myths as allegory as part of their arguments. Even if he acknowledged a supernatural order, the character of Socrates in Plato's dialogues was critical of the morality of conventional gods. The Stoics believed that logic and reason could reconcile different beliefs with the underlying meanings of myths.

I really hope that these additional dimensions shed some light on how mythology was intertwined with a wide variety of religious practices in ancient Greek civilization. Please let me know if there is any portion that needs to be elaborated upon more.

Cults of the Hero

After their valiant acts, several historical individuals like as Brasidas and Achilles, amongst others, inspired a modest amount of local adoration. Their cults erected shrines to them and celebrated their glory with rites and games.

Myths Regarding the Underworld and the Afterlife

The ancient Greeks had the belief that after death, the soul traveled to the land of Hades. Mythical travelers such as Odysseus had a glimpse of the bliss of Elysium or the endless torture of Tartarus. The river Styx served as a wall to separate the gloomy underworld from the surface world.

Astronomy and Mythology

Some constellations have been given fantastical backstories, such as the legend of Cassiopeia's Queen being entombed among the stars. Along with its mythological connotations, the night sky provided those Greeks interested in astronomy with a wealth of information.

The Function of Theatre

Dramatizations written by Aeschylus, Sophocles, and Euripides had a significant impact on the ways in which myths were understood and preserved for posterity. Their misfortunes breathed vivid new life into the stories that were told on stage.

Myths Local to the Area

Despite the dominance of the Olympians, there were also regional deities, such as Athena, who was highly worshipped since she was the patron goddess of mighty Athens. Myths also gave heroes a heightened position in the cities in which they were born and raised.

A Heritage in Rome

When the Romans adopted Greek civilization, they also adopted Greek deities into their own pantheon. Zeus was elevated to the position of Jupiter, while Aphrodite was elevated to the position of Venus. Myths continued to spread over the broad territory of the Roman Empire.

Primary Sources for the Myths

When one delves into the realm of ancient myths, they are instantly immersed in an enthralling universe filled with gods, goddesses, heroes, monsters, and stories of extraordinary beings. It is essential, however, to investigate these stories' basic sources in order to have a complete understanding and appreciation of them. This investigation of the primary sources, which includes documents, artifacts, and narratives, will provide a more in-depth comprehension of the cultural, historical, and literary settings.

Myths can have a variety of origins, which change depending on the society and era in question. The writings of Homer, Hesiod, and the Tragedians are considered to be the primary texts for the study of Greek mythology. Homer is responsible for the epic poems "Iliad" and "Odyssey," both of which describe the account of the Trojan War and its aftermath. These poems provide an introduction to a great number of the gods and heroes of Greek mythology, as well as everlasting lessons on valor, honor, and the human condition.

The "Theogony" of Hesiod is yet another important source for Greek mythology. It gives a comprehensive explanation of how the universe was created as well as the family trees of the gods. The book "Works and Days" by Hesiod is also very important; it is a collection of moral and practical counsel for life that is interlaced with mythical stories.

Through their dramatic works, the tragedians such as Aeschylus, Sophocles, and Euripides contributed to the expansion of Greek mythology. Mythic stories were frequently recounted and reinterpreted in these dramas, which offered viewers fresh points of view as well as greater insights into the individuals and the forces that drove them.

On the other hand, Virgil, Ovid, and Livy are the authors most responsible for the development of Roman mythology. The "Aeneid" written by Virgil recounts the tale of Aeneas, a Trojan hero who was also an ancestor of the people who founded Rome. It is a story that mirrors the growth of Rome itself, and it is an epic narrative of struggle, sacrifice, and destiny.

The "Metamorphoses" of Ovid is a compilation of more than 250 mythical tales that have been woven into a continuous narrative that begins with the creation of the universe and ends with the deification of Julius Caesar. Ovid wrote the "Metamorphoses" in the first century BC. Although it is essentially a chronicle of factual events, Livy's "History of Rome" also contains a number of myths and stories related to Rome's earlier days.

Both the Poetic Edda and the Prose Edda were created in the 13th century, but they were based on older oral and written sources. These two books are considered to be the fundamental sources for Norse mythology. These books discuss a broad variety of Norse myths, such as the origin of the universe, the exploits of gods and heroes, and the eschatological event known as Ragnarök, which is a prophecy regarding the end of the world.

The examination of primary sources requires the use of a critical eye. It is essential to keep in mind that these sources were frequently products of their time and reflected the ideas, values, and prejudices of the society in which they were created as well as the people who created them. As such, it is important that they be read within the framework of their own cultural and historical settings.

Comparing the findings of several different sources is another useful strategy. Myths that are narrated in a similar fashion but by various civilizations or in different books can each give their own distinct viewpoints and interpretations. The universal attraction of these ageless tales may be better understood through comparative research since it sheds light on human experiences and problems that are shared across time and space.

Your experience will be significantly improved if you have even a fundamental comprehension of the language used in these sources. Although English translations are easily available, it is possible that they miss some of the subtleties present in the languages from which they were derived. Your ability to comprehend anything on a deeper level can be enhanced by even the most fundamental knowledge of Greek, Latin, or Old Norse.

Last but not least, keep in mind that the study of myths is about more than just comprehending the past. Myths continue to have a significant impact on our art, literature, philosophy, and even our day-to-day language. As you explore further into these key sources, you'll begin to notice their impacts popping up in unexpected places. Writers, artists, and anybody else interested in investigating humanity's collective history can draw inspiration from them in a rich and plentiful manner.

When thinking about animals from mythology, it's intriguing to explore how such creatures have developed in our collective imagination over the course of the ages. For example, in Western mythology, dragons are frequently portrayed as terrifying, fire-breathing monsters who stand for anarchy and devastation. Dragons, on the other hand, are seen as beings of good fortune and intelligence in Eastern civilizations such as China. These societies equate dragons with water and fertility. Primary texts frequently offer the first portrayals of these animals, so laying the groundwork for their development in subsequent mythology and popular culture. This contrast between Eastern and Western dragons highlights the varying ways in which different cultures interpret and represent identical mythical themes, which in turn enriches our understanding of mythology from all around the world.

Primary Source Analysis and Interpretation

The challenge of deciphering myths from their main sources can be a difficult one. It is absolutely necessary to take into consideration the figurative language and other literary methods that are utilized in these writings. For example, in Greek mythology, the sea is frequently seen as a sign of disorder and the unknown, whereas the sky is seen as a representation of order and divinity. Your comprehension of the stories and the ideas they represent can be improved by being familiar with the symbols used in them.

In addition, several myths are connected to one another, and the same characters and events can be found in more than one story. When you look at information from a variety of sources, you may construct a picture that is more accurate and complete of the mythical world and the people who live in it. For example, reading Homer's "Odyssey" as well as Hesiod's "Theogony" can provide you with a more well-rounded understanding of the personality of Zeus, the monarch of the Greek gods.

Mythology and Social Structure

The original origins of myths offer illuminating information about the communities that were responsible for their creation. Myths frequently reflect the social standards, ethical ideals, religious beliefs, and historical events that were prevalent during the eras in which they were created. For instance, the heroic ideals depicted in Homer's "Iliad" represent the warrior culture of ancient Greece, while the protagonists in Sophocles' plays encounter moral conundrums that emphasize the ethical discussions of the time period.

Myths, on the Other Hand, and the Individual

The study of myths may provide important insights into human nature as well as the common experiences shared by all humans. Myths are stories that have been told for generations and may be read by people of all ages and cultures because they cover universal topics such as love, loss, bravery, and the search for meaning. The exploration of these tales may lead to introspection and development on a personal level, making the study of myths a worthwhile activity not just from an academic standpoint, but also on a personal one.

Myths in the Context of Modern Life

Myths, despite their antiquity, continue to hold a place in today's culture for a variety of reasons. They serve as a source of motivation for works of modern literature, film, and other kinds of current media. Your appreciation for these contemporary retellings might be heightened by gaining an understanding of the original sources from which these stories originated.

For instance, having a deeper appreciation for Marvel's Thor comics and movies might result from having a better grasp of the original Norse stories. In a similar vein, having a background in Greek mythology might enrich your experience of reading Rick Riordan's Percy Jackson series or watching movies like "Clash of the Titans."

Cultural Syncretism and Swapping of Traditions

Last but not least, engaging in research into original sources can bring to light remarkable examples of cultural mixing and blending. A great number of myths were taken with conquerors or transported along trade routes, and as a result, they were altered by a variety of various civilizations. For instance, a significant number of Roman myths are simply retold copies of Greek stories. In a similar manner, Buddhist tales originating in India were absorbed into the mythology of both China and Japan. These interactions between people of different cultures shed light on the interrelated nature of human communities throughout history.

The Phoenix is a powerful example of how culture is passed down from generation to generation in the domain of legendary beings. This mythical bird is mentioned in the legends of the Greeks, Romans, Egyptians, Chinese, and Japanese. It is a symbol of rebirth and regeneration. various religious beliefs and philosophical ideas are reflected in the many various ways that it is shown throughout different civilizations.

As you continue to investigate original sources of myths, keep in mind that you should approach them with an open mind and a sense of genuine curiosity. Each myth provides a distinct glimpse into the human imagination as well as the never-ending journey to comprehend the universe and where we fit into it.

Chapter 2: The Gods and Goddesses

Cosmogony: Origins of the Universe

Mythology in ancient Greece offered solutions for basic concerns that continue to interest modern humans, such as what caused the planet and the universe to come into being. Poets were responsible for the development of creation tales, which in turn influenced Greek cosmology and the genealogy of the gods.

Hesiod's Theogony is considered to be one of the oldest narratives, and it begins by imagining chaos as the emptiness that existed before all else. Gaia, the world, and some of the earth's progeny, such as the gloomy halls of Tartarus, evolved from the disorder that existed before. As did other early divinities, Gaia gave birth to her children by means of parthenogenesis. She gave birth to Uranus, the sky, who in turn fertilized Gaia, which resulted in the birth of oceans and mountains rich in fertility.

The Cyclopes and the Hectohenries, who were later children of Uranus and Gaia, posed a challenge to Uranus' authority, so he exiled them to the underworld of Tartarus. This infuriated Gaia, so she fashioned a massive sickle with flint blades and persuaded her younger sons to perform the castration on their father. Erinyes, giants, and ash trees all sprang from the blood of Uranus that was spilled onto Gaia. His genitalia gave birth to the goddess Aphrodite, who emerged from the water to signal the beginning of a golden period.

Cronus, the eldest son of Gaia and Uranus, was the most powerful of their children and eventually conquered his father with the assistance of his mother. He ruled at a prosperous time until his son Zeus overthrew him and took his throne. After Zeus had successfully subdued the Titans and other cosmic powers, he ruled the cosmos from atop Mount Olympus and created the Olympian order.

These legendary accounts attempted to provide answers to important issues about the cosmos by endowing the gods with complex family trees and distinct personas. Myths were given a symbolic reinterpretation by later philosophers, who saw primal energies like as Eros, Gaia, and in them. However, in the eyes of the ancients, these stories were deep allegories that positioned Greek culture inside the divine framework of the world itself.

Several fascinating nuggets of supplementary information on Greek cosmological myths:

According to Hesiod, the condition of chaos in its original, undeveloped form existed concurrently with other fundamental ideas such as darkness, earth, love, and struggle. Over the course of time, these have converged into characteristics that we are familiar with.

In certain versions of the creation story, the original differentiation of the cosmos, earth, and sky was credited to various individuals, such as Uranus, Gaea's son, or the androgynous primal deity Ophion.

The ritual of castrating Uranus and the subsequent creation of gods from his blood served as a symbolic explanation for the order in which abilities were passed down in heaven and on earth.

Cronus ruled throughout a pseudo-historical Golden Age until he was dethroned by his son Zeus in a heavenly succession that echoed, on a smaller scale, Jupiter's rise in popularity among the Romans.

The conflict between Zeus and Typhon, a huge snake, was symbolic of the triumph of order over anarchy, as was Zeus' eventual victory over the monster Typhon. This made Zeus' authority that stronger.

There are still blank spots in our understanding of the meaning of fundamental ideas like Nyx, Chaos, and Tartarus, which had philosophical and religious repercussions in the past.

Later Orphic traditions built on cosmic cycles of creation and destruction as well as the transmigration of souls in ways that may have been similar to those of other religions.

Plato and other philosophers suggested allegorical interpretations, in which the characters of myths symbolically represented deeper philosophical realities that extended beyond their literal beginnings.

The Titans

Titans have been a subject of fascination for humans for millennia since they are depicted as imposing individuals who wield enormous power and influence. By making appearances in a wide variety of works of literature, art, and popular culture, the primal gods of Greek mythology have permanently etched themselves into our collective consciousness. Learning about the Titans in Greek mythology and their place in the cosmic order of that culture's mythology can provide us some fascinating insights into ancient Greek society as well as the human condition.

Understanding the Roles of the Titans

The Titans were the offspring of the god Uranus (Sky) and the goddess Gaia (Earth), and they embodied different characteristics of the natural world. Oceanus, Coeus, Crius, Hyperion, Iapetus, Theia, Rhea, Themis, Mnemosyne, Phoebe, and Tethys were the original twelve Titans, together with the dreaded Cronus. Tethys was the only Titan who had a daughter. Everyone ruled over their own territory. For instance, the river that encircled the planet was connected with Oceanus, whereas the light of heaven was identified with Hyperion.

It is essential to keep in mind that the Titans were not only personifications of different types of natural occurrences. They were multidimensional characters, each with their own personalities, connections, and stories to tell. As such, we might consider them to be incarnations of the ancient Greeks' knowledge of the cosmos as well as the human situation.

The Titanomachy and the Reign of Cronus in Greek Mythology

Cronus, the Titan who was the youngest but also the most renowned, was their leader. After he had Uranus, his father, deposed, he ascended to the position of monarch of the cosmos. However, because of a prophecy that stated he would be deposed by one of his own children, Cronus ate his children as soon as they were born. This was done out of terror. This heinous crime laid the groundwork for his demise and paved the way for the Olympic gods to come to power.

The Titanomachy was an epic battle that lasted for 10 years and was the culmination of a fight between Cronus and Zeus, Cronus' son. This cosmic conflict brought an end to the reign of the Titans and heralded the beginning of the dominance of the Olympians. In Greek mythology, the Titanomachy is a crucial event that symbolizes the shift from an ancient order that was more chaotic to a new order that is more organized.

In post-Hesiodic literature, the titans play an important role.

In later Greek literature, the portrayal of the Titans underwent a progression. Titans were frequently presented in a more empathetic light in the works of playwrights such as Aeschylus and Euripides, among others. For instance, the Titan Prometheus, who was of the second generation, was considered a hero of humanity because of the story that he stole fire from the gods and gave it to people. Prometheus became a symbol of rebellion, intellect, and development as a result of his act of defiance against the Olympian gods.

Closer to the Titans Than Ever Before

Reading about the Titans may teach current readers a great deal that is useful in everyday life. They are a representation of the ancient Greeks' concept of the universe and the state of humans. In addition, the tales that surround the Titans examine universal topics such as power, defiance, justice, and the repetitive cycle of time.

When conducting research on the Titans, it is best to begin with original materials, such as Hesiod's "Theogony." This epic poem offers the most in-depth and detailed description of the Titans' ancestry as well as their place in the natural order of the universe. In addition, the writings of Homer, Aeschylus, and other ancient authors can provide you with a more comprehensive understanding of the Titans and the role they played in Greek mythology.

It is important to bear in mind that although if English translations of these materials are easily accessible, it is possible that they do not convey all of the complexity of the original Greek text. As a result, having even a little comprehension of ancient Greek might significantly improve one's capacity to comprehend these narratives.

Also take into consideration the historical and cultural background of these tales. The ideals, beliefs, and concerns of ancient Greek society are reflected in the Titans and in the stories that surround them. You may obtain a more in-depth understanding of ancient Greek culture and the influence that it had on Western civilization if you examine these tales and place them in the appropriate perspective.

As part of your investigation of the Titans, you could also be interested in looking into how they are portrayed in contemporary writing and other forms of popular culture. Titans and their mythology continue to inspire and resound with audiences of today, as seen by works as diverse as Mary Shelley's "Frankenstein" and the "God of War" video game series.

Exploring the realm of the Titans is similar to going on an exciting adventure deep beyond the reaches of the human imagination. You will discover important truths about the world, mankind, and yourself as you delve further into their narratives. And maybe, just like Prometheus, you'll stumble upon a glimmer of heavenly fire that will shed light on your own journey.

There is a fascinating connection to be made between the Titans and astrology when seen from that angle. Mythology was the means through which the ancient Greeks attempted to make sense of the natural world and the mysteries of the cosmos. The Titans, who embodied a variety of cosmic and earthly forces, were essential players in the interpretation of celestial events due to the fact that they were the source of all these components. For example, the god Cronus, who was related to the passage of time, was also identified with the planet Saturn. In contemporary astrology, Saturn is still associated with concepts like as time, self-discipline, and learning, which is a strong echo of the legendary counterpart of this planet. This remarkable confluence between mythology and astrology further emphasizes the ever-present significance of the Titans in our comprehension of the universe and of ourselves.

The Titan Prometheus is known for his forward thinking.

In the realm of the Titans, Prometheus is a pivotal person. He is renowned for his knowledge and for being a benefactor to humanity. It is well known that he deceived Zeus for the sake of humanity by ensuring that people received the best portion of animal sacrifices while the gods received the less desirable portions of the animals. Prometheus is famous for taking fire from the gods and delivering it to humans. This deed is interpreted as a metaphor for the awakening of human consciousness and the beginning of civilization.

The myth of Prometheus also includes a significant investigation of the concepts of suffering and perseverance. After Prometheus stole fire from Zeus, Zeus punished him by chaining him to a rock and having an eagle devour his liver every day. Prometheus's liver would regenerate each night, but it would still be eaten the next day. Prometheus, despite his suffering, would not give in to Zeus's demands, thereby personifying defiance in the face of oppression and inequality.

The enduring titan is known as Atlas.

As a kind of retribution for his participation in the Titanomachy, Zeus sentenced another notable Titan known as Atlas to bear the weight of the heavens on his shoulders. This picture of Atlas, the giant stoically suffering his eternal punishment, has become a potent icon in the culture of the Western world, embodying endurance, strength, and the human capacity to face hardship in its various forms.

The Titanesses were mighty female deities in mythology.

The female Titans, often known as Titanesses, had important duties to perform as well. For instance, Themis, the Titaness who was responsible for maintaining heavenly law and order, served as a counselor to Zeus and was held in very high regard by the other gods. Despite the fact that Gaia was a primordial deity and not a Titaness in the strictest sense, she was venerated as the embodiment of Earth since she was the mother of the Titans.

The Titans' Influence and Its Consequences

The Titans have left an enduring impact in a variety of modern society's sectors and facets, and this legacy will continue for generations to come. For example, the name of the element titanium comes from the Titans, which is a sign of the metal's power and longevity because titanium is named after them. The tale of Oedipus, the tragic Greek hero who was the grandson of the Titan Iapetus, is where Sigmund Freud got the idea for the word "Oedipus complex," which was first used in the field of psychology.

Additionally, the Titans continue to serve as a source of inspiration for works of current literature, art, and entertainment. They are frequently reinvented in ways that are relatable to contemporary audiences and appear in works of fantasy literature, comic comics, video games, and films. The Titans' evergreen popularity is evidence of the widespread and enduring significance they hold in our culture.

The Ancient Greek Gods and Philosophical Ideas

There is also a philosophical perspective that may be applied to the interpretation of the Titan mythology. For instance, the narrative of the Titanomachy can be seen as a metaphor for the conflict between order, which is symbolized by the Olympians, and chaos, which is symbolized by the Titans. The struggle between order and chaos is a recurrent topic in a wide variety of mythologies and philosophical systems. It reflects a core component of the human experience.

The Afterthought of Epimetheus

Epimetheus, who is Prometheus's brother, is a fascinating Titan in his own right. In contrast to Prometheus, whose name means "forethought," his name implies "afterthought" or "late thinker." His role is to serve as a counterweight to Prometheus. Epimetheus is well known for his part in the creation of Pandora, the first woman, by the gods as part of their retaliation against mankind for Prometheus's theft of fire. Pandora was one of the consequences for Epimetheus's actions. In spite of his brother's caution not to accept any gifts from the gods, Epimetheus fell in love with Pandora's beauty and decided to marry her, accidentally introducing worries and sufferings (Pandora's "box") into the world in the process.

Metis, also known as The Wise Counsel,

Metis, a Titaness of the second generation, was famed for her knowledge and was regarded to be the personification of cunning intellect, also known as "Metis." She was Zeus's first spouse, and according to the Greek mythology, she was the one who provided him with the wisdom he required to destroy his father, Cronus. In addition, it was foretold that she would give birth to children who were very powerful, which is another reason why Zeus chose to consume her: he did not want his dominion to be challenged by her progeny. However, their daughter Athena, who is the goddess of knowledge as well as strategic battle, finally emerged fully grown from Zeus's skull, which suggests that wisdom can never be completely controlled or suppressed.

The Godlike Beings Known as the Titans and the Natural World
The Titans had a profound connection to the natural world, and their myths were frequently utilized to shed light on many aspects of the natural world. For instance, the Titan Hyperion, who personified light, was the father of the deities Helios (Sun), Selene (Moon), and Eos (Dawn). Additionally, Oceanus symbolized the river that encircled the earth, while Tethys was linked with the characteristics of water that made it productive and provided life.

The Titans and Their Relation to Astronomy

Astronomy is another field that has been significantly influenced by the Titans. The Titans have inspired the naming of a significant number of the moons that orbit the planets in our solar system. Tethys, Phoebe, and Hyperion are just a few of the Titans whose names have been given to several of Saturn's moons. Saturn is the Roman counterpart of the Greek god Cronus. The name Titan was given to Saturn's moon Titan because it is the biggest moon in the system.

The Giants of the Art World

Throughout history, the topic of the Titans has been a favorite one for artists to depict in their work. Particularly noteworthy is the fact that their conflict with the Olympians during the Titanomachy has been memorialized in a great number of sculptures, paintings, and frescoes. The torment that was inflicted upon Atlas and Prometheus has also been extensively portrayed in a broad variety of creative genres, often as a means of meditating on the concepts of perseverance and defiance.

The Titans in Various Works of Literature

In many works of literature, the Titans frequently represent either the powers of nature, the strength of the primeval world, or revolt against the rule of the gods. The tales of the Titans have served as a wellspring of creativity for writers throughout the ages, providing them with the impetus to investigate topics such as authority, equity, and the nature of the human condition.

The Great Books and the Contemporary Lexicon

Even the vocabulary we use now shows evidence of the Titans' enduring impact. Titanic refers to something that is huge in size, strength, or power and gets its name from the ancient Greek mythological race known as the Titans. Similarly, the term "Promethean" refers to deeds that are daring, inventive, or proudly autonomous; these traits are reflective of Prometheus's character.

The Titans have made a major contribution to the field of psychology through their many accomplishments. For instance, the notion of the "Promethean complex" has been offered to explain a psychological condition in which an individual challenges authority or cultural standards, driven by a conviction in their own exceptionalism. This concept is similar to that of the "Oedipus complex" or the "Electra complex," which have also been presented.

As a last point of discussion, it should be mentioned that the Titans' influence has spread into the realm of biotechnology. Titan cells are a special kind of fungal cell that get its name from the fact that they are far larger than the majority of other fungal cells. This is an obvious allusion to the titans from Greek mythology.

As a result, the Titans' legacy can be seen in a variety of fields, ranging from culture to science. This serves as a witness to the essential role that the Titans played in mythology as well as its continuous significance in contemporary times.

In order to dig even deeper into the realm of the Titans, it is worthwhile to investigate their Roman analogues, who are known as the Titans in Roman mythology. In spite of the fact that the Romans adopted and adapted Greek mythology, their depictions of these primordial entities were distinct from those seen in Greek mythology. For example, the Roman god Saturn, who was considered to be the equivalent of the Greek god Cronus, was honored during the festival of Saturnalia. This was a time of merriment and the subversion of social conventions, which was a far cry from Cronus' reputation as a terrifying figure in Greek mythology. When these nuances are understood, a more complex and nuanced view on the Titans and the continuing effect they have had throughout civilizations may be gained.

The Olympians: Main Greek Gods and Goddesses

Greek mythology is an intricate web of stories and characters that has had a significant impact on Western culture in a myriad of different ways. The Olympians, who were the primary gods who were said to have reigned from their heavenly home atop Mount Olympus, are the primary focus of these legends. This chapter will give a thorough introduction to these gods and goddesses, including historical context as well as contemporary interpretations of their myths and stories.

Zeus is known as the King of the Gods.

Zeus, the Olympian deity of the sky and thunder, is perhaps the one that people know the most about. He was the son of the Titans Cronus and Rhea, and he successfully led his brothers in a rebellion against their dictatorial father. He was also known as Prometheus. Zeus, in his role as king of the gods, presided over all matters pertaining to law and justice, rendering definitive judgments and ensuring that order was preserved.

Hera was a goddess associated with marriage.

Hera, who was married to Zeus, was a goddess who presided over marriage, motherhood, and women. In spite of the fact that she was the queen of the gods, Hera's union to Zeus was everything but happy because the deity was frequently unfaithful to his wife. Hera frequently sought retribution against Zeus's lovers and the offspring they bore, and her myths frequently featured themes related to jealousy and wrath.

Poseidon is known as the "God of the Sea."

Another of Zeus's brothers, Poseidon, was given authority over the oceans. When he became enraged, he was a strong god who was also known to have a short fuse. He was responsible for earthquakes. It was well known that Poseidon had a competitive spirit, as he memorably exhibited when he competed with Athena for patronage over the city of Athens. Poseidon ultimately lost to Athena.

Athena, often known as the Goddess of Wisdom

Athena, daughter of Zeus, was a Greek goddess associated with bravery, intelligence, and the art of strategic warfare. She was Zeus's favorite kid and was born fully armed from his forehead. She was also his favorite child. Athena was honored as the patron goddess of Athens since she was the one who presented the city with its most famous tree—the olive tree.

The Greek goddess of love and beauty is known as Aphrodite.

After Cronus castrated his father Uranus and hurled his genitals into the water, the sea foam gave birth to the goddess Aphrodite, who is the personification of love, beauty, and fertility. Aphrodite had the power to make gods and mortals alike fall in love, which frequently resulted in both a romantic atmosphere and anarchy.

The Greek gods Apollo and Artemis were known as "The Twin Archers."

Both Apollo and Artemis were identical twins and were born to Zeus and Leto as their offspring. Apollo was the god of music, healing, and prophecy, while Artemis was the goddess of the hunt, the wilderness, and chastity. Apollo was worshiped in ancient Greece. Both of them were accomplished archers, and during their lifetimes, they frequently collaborated with one another.

Hephaestus was known as the Divine Smith, and Ares was known as the God of War.

Hera was the one who gave birth to Hephaestus; hence Zeus was not involved in the process of his birth. Hephaestus was the god of fire and blacksmiths. He was married to Aphrodite, and the focus of many of his tales is on his talent as a craftsman as well as the turbulent nature of his marriage. Ares, the Greek god of war, personified the bloody and unbridled sides of battle, which stood in stark contrast to Athena's methodical approach to dispute resolution.

Demeter and Persephone are often referred to as the "Mother-Daughter Duo."

A captivating mother-daughter story is told about the Greek goddesses Demeter, who is associated with agriculture, and Persephone, who reigns in the underworld. The traditional myth that explains natural occurrences is the narrative of Persephone being kidnapped by Hades, the god of the underworld, and how Demeter's grief is responsible for the changing of the seasons.

Hermes was known as "the Messenger of the Gods" in ancient times.

Hermes, the son of Zeus and the nymph Maia, served as the divine messenger and was also revered as the patron deity of commerce, thieves, and travel. Hermes, who was famous for his craftiness and shrewdness, was Zeus' herald and functioned as the god's personal assistant.

Hades is the name of the god who rules the underworld.

Even though he was not one of the twelve Olympians in the traditional sense, Hades maintained a great amount of authority as the god of death and the king of the underworld. Due to the fact that he was associated with death and the afterlife, many other gods and mortals regarded him with a great deal of horror.

These gods had an impact on every aspect of life in ancient Greece, from the government and social order to the agricultural practices and the shifting of the seasons. Even in this day and age, their stories continue to reverberate, infusing contemporary literature, cinema, and art with evergreen ideas of authority, love, and retribution, as well as wisdom. In the next part, we will investigate the cultural and historical relevance of the Olympians in greater depth, as well as their portrayals in a variety of types of media.

The significance of the Olympians from a cultural and historical perspective.

The stories, qualities, and rituals that surrounded the Olympian gods had a significant impact on ancient Greek civilization, helping to establish the norms, values, and institutions that persisted during that era. Temples that were devoted to the gods served as holy places for worship and were frequently the locations of significant events that took place inside the city-state. Through prayer and sacrifice, the ancient Greeks attempted to win over the favor of their gods in the hopes of securing their blessing on anything from successful military battles to prosperous agricultural endeavors.

The Panhellenic Games, which included the Olympic Games that were held in Zeus's honor, were an important cultural event that brought together athletes and spectators from all across the Greek world. Other ceremonies and celebrations, such as those known as the Eleusinian Mysteries and which were devoted to the goddesses Demeter and Persephone, held significant religious importance and guaranteed participants a more satisfying afterlife.

Representations of That Thing in Art and Literature

Both in ancient times and in modern times, several works of art and literature have been created using the Olympians as their subject matter. In ancient Greek pottery, sculpture, and architecture, the gods frequently figure in scenes from their tales. These images portray a variety of human experiences, including love and conflict, as well as joy and mourning.

The Homeric epics "Iliad" and "Odyssey" include some of the oldest and most important depictions of the Olympians in written form. Both of these works are considered to be examples of "epic literature." The gods participate actively in the story by directing, assisting, or hindering the human protagonists in various ways.

In today's world, the Olympians continue to serve as a source of creativity, making appearances everywhere from the world of high literature to that of popular culture. They play a significant role in works written for young adults like as the "Percy Jackson" series written by Rick Riordan, as well as films such as Disney's "Hercules," and video games such as "God of War."

The Athletes of Ancient Greece in Today's World

Even in a purportedly contemporary and secular society, the Olympians continue to have a significant amount of influence. They are alluded to in the names of planetary bodies and moons, brands and enterprises, as well as conceptual frameworks and theoretical frameworks in the scientific community. For instance, the phrase "herculean," which refers to an activity that requires a considerable deal of power or effort, was borrowed from the demi-god Hercules, who was known in Greek as Heracles.

The Olympic Champions and Ancient Rome

Beyond the borders of Greece, the Olympians exerted their influence. The Romans were exposed to Greek culture, and as a result, they adopted some of the Greek gods into their own pantheon, although with a few modifications. The gods were known by their Roman names and were frequently worshiped in settings that were uniquely Roman. For instance, the goddess Athena was renamed Minerva, which allowed her to retain her affiliation with intellect while also having a connection to commerce and the arts.

The Olympians and Their Meaning in Today's World

The tales of the Olympians provide modern readers with a plethora of different metaphorical and allegorical interpretations to choose from. They are everlasting touchstones for examining our own lives since they include essential aspects of human existence, such as experiences and worries.

The Olympians also bring to mind the efforts made by ancient people to comprehend and make sense of the world around them. They give human characteristics and natural forces a persona, providing a glimpse into the way ancient Greeks attempted to make sense of the world around them.

Finally, the Olympians present us with a challenge through the moral ambiguity that they embody. They exhibit a range of behaviors, some of which are commendable while others are abhorrent, which compels us to wrestle with the complexities of right and wrong, fairness and injustice, love and hatred.

Hestia is known as the Goddess of the Home and Hearth.

Hestia, the goddess of the hearth, home, and domestic life, was listed as one of the twelve Olympians in the first list that was compiled of the gods of Olympia. It was believed that she was a kind and non-confrontational divinity due to the fact that, like Athena and Artemis, she was a virgin goddess. Because of her important position in both home life and hospitality, Hestia was always given the first offering during the annual household sacrifice. Dionysus, on the other hand, took her position in subsequent lists, which may indicate a shift in either the ideals of society or the actions of religious institutions.

An examination of Greek mythology may be made more interesting and illuminating by focusing on the Olympians because of the unique personalities, varied realms, and dramatic storylines associated with each of them. They offer a vivid perspective through which to observe the world of the ancients, and they continue to motivate and perplex us in our day and age. Their narratives, which are brimming with symbolism and meaning, serve as a timely reminder of the everlasting power of myth to mold, mirror, and test our knowledge of the wider world. When learning about the Olympians, it's important to also pay attention to their Roman equivalents. The Roman pantheon was based on the Greek one, although the Romans added several adjustments to it. For example, the Greek god Ares was seen to be a destructive and unstable force, but his Roman equivalent, Mars, was regarded in a more favorable light since he was considered to be the father of the Roman nation and was seen as a symbol of heroism in battle. These variances provide for an interesting study of how many societies might view the same deities in light of their own morals and expectations of how society should function as a whole.

Other Deities

The ancient Greek religion contained a wide range of additional significant deities in addition to the twelve Olympians. These minor gods and goddesses frequently presided over particular kingdoms or locations, and they contributed variety to the pantheon's intricate structure.

The following are some important statistics:

- Hades is known as the Lord of the Underworld. He is the eldest of his siblings, yet he was given the role of Ruler of the Realm of the Dead.

- Hestia, the goddess of the house and the equilibrium of the family, chose to abstain from sexual activity so that she might maintain her impartial status.

- Hecate, the towering goddess of sorcery, witchcraft, and crossroads, is revered at the edges of the night.

-Morpheus, the creator of dreams and visions who received their inspiration from Hypnos, the deity of sleep.

-Pan, the deity of the countryside and wild places, is seen here in his human and goat forms, enjoying themselves to the fullest.

-Dionysus, who was a mortal in the beginning but was raised to godhood, was the god of ecstasy and brought it to the world via his gifts of wine, frenzy, and theater.

- the Moirai, also known as the Fates, who governed the course of mortal existence from birth to death.

- the Litai who made up for wrongs by praying for remorse at shrines.
- With unyielding fury, the Furies (Erinyes) punished unlawful blood crimes such as murder and matricide.

- Eros was the personification of love in its most fundamental form, both in its sexual and romantic expressions and in its filial and maternal guises.

- The Parcae were goddesses who were visible beyond Olympus and who were responsible for spinning, measuring, and cutting the lifelines of mortals.

- Hecate was given a significant role in many heretical witchcraft traditions that survived into the Christian era.

- Hermes was considered to be the psychopomp between the worlds. He was also considered to be the patron saint of travelers, hospitality, and diplomacy.

- Charon, who was in charge of transporting souls, and Cerberus, who was in charge of guarding the gate to Hades, were both minor underworld deities.

- Gods with notoriously phallic shapes, such as Priapus, were primarily responsible for ensuring the fertility of cattle and crops.

- River gods were discussed, such as Achelous, who was known for his role as the wine-bearing father of Dionysus.

- Monsters were the personification of wild forces, like as Typhon and Echidna, who were ultimately vanquished by gods and heroes.

- The seductive sounds of sirens, which emanated from female bodies that were entangled with birds and other marine creatures, were said to have led seafarers astray and into danger.

Lesser divinities typically had characteristics that varied from place to place, and they created intricate patronage webs with heroes, locations, and families. These webs of patronage spread the variety of Greek pantheism across the Hellenic globe. There were other nymphs that were related to specific locations, such as oreads living in mountains and nereids swimming among the waves of the ocean.

In addition, after achieving apotheosis within cults, heroes may take on divine responsibilities of a lesser nature. Creatures on the brink of divinity often combined human and animal characteristics.

In general, Greece's wide variety in topography and ways of life gave rise to a profusion of regionally specific gods and goddesses. Their depth adds a layer of complexity to societal systems while also serving as a reflection of humanity's connection to the natural environment. Because of their sheer numbers, the overarching religious traditions of Hellas guaranteed that no area ever felt under-represented therein.

Chapter 3: Heroes and Demigods

The Concept of Heroism in Ancient Greece

Heroes held a role in ancient Greek culture and mythology that was one of great respect and affection for the people of that time period. Beyond the realm of eternal deities, heroes represented the aspirational characteristics and traits that citizens aspired to have. They were exemplars of bravery, strength, and selfless sacrifice based on moral principles. Their enduring tales continue to attract us even in this day and age.

In ancient Greek tradition, a hero was someone who arose from a divine-mortal lineage, possessed remarkable powers, and utilized those abilities for the good of mankind while battling dangerous adversaries. Heroes were sometimes driven to undertake risky travels by a desire for honor or a vow of revenge. These voyages required them to face innumerable risks with cunning and fortitude, yet they were undeterred. They gained an immortality of reputation in the minds of people of subsequent generations as a result of their extraordinary achievements.

However, beyond their brave deeds, heroes sometimes displayed human weaknesses that served as lessons for readers to avoid making the same mistakes. When the son of the deity Heracles went insane and caused destruction to cities, it brought to light the fact that even the most powerful beings are susceptible to divine influence or the madness that may cause reason to fail. We are reminded of the responsibility that comes along with advancing technology by mementos of Dedalus's ambitious project, which resulted in the death of his own child.

The complicated efforts of these multi-dimensional figures to strike a balance between grandeur and fragility constituted captivating mirrors for the Greeks to see their own inner strengths and failings reflected onto. Their footprints on the regions they explored and the foes they defeated were recorded in oral narratives that augmented their living legacy. These accounts inspired subsequent societies and continue to be astonishingly relevant in our present world. Acts of perseverance in nobility, compassion, and justice in the face of life's challenges are examples of the heroic qualities that continue to inspire people and call mankind toward attaining its fullest potential. Their stories have stood the test of time because they demonstrate how even regular people may achieve remarkable accomplishments by calling upon the inner grandeur of their soul.

The following are examples of core Greek principles that were highlighted and developed via the stories of mythological heroes:

- Hubris vs. Humility - Stories of Icarus caution against excessive pride, which leads to fall, and emphasize the importance of maintaining adequate modesty.

- Justice and the Law - The gods stood for moral order, while heroes protected the cosmos by taking a stance against oppression and wrongdoing in order to establish righteousness.

- Obligation to One's Family and Community - Many legendary figures, like as Theseus, risked their lives to protect their towns and families, placing a premium on familial relationships and community well-being.

- Figures like Odysseus displayed phronesis, also known as practical intelligence, above brashness by employing sensible planning, and this was a demonstration of both wisdom and moderation.

- Heroes gladly submitted themselves to adversity for the sake of a higher cause, knowing that the heroic deeds they performed would result in the bestowment of benefits on their respective lands.

- Myths about hospitality involved characters opening their homes to deities posing as outsiders as a test of Xenia, an essential component of society.

- Athletics and Arete - The excellence of the hero's performance in athletics and accomplishments revealed the growth of virtue that is treasured by poleis.

- Fate and Free Will - The stories called into doubt Moirai's plans, but they still offered possibility for heroism via stubborn human decision in the face of restrictions.

- The Afterlife/Death - Passages into Hades' Realms Symbolized Hope in Legacy/Eternal Remembrance Crossings into Hades' realms represented the inevitability of one's own mortality.

Additional characteristics of heroism in the mythology of ancient Greece:

- It was common for heroes to have a divine parent (often the father), which endowed them with semi-divine talents and suggested that they were destined for a great destiny.

- A great number of heroes were required by the gods to demonstrate their worthiness by enduring arduous "labors" or tests. Both Heracles and Jason are renowned for completing a great number of labors.

- It was absolutely essential to display bravery in combat. Heroes were lauded for their prowess in combat and their ability to vanquish evil creatures. They often battled on behalf of towns or kingdoms.

- Heroic voyages of self-discovery were expressed in quests for significant artifacts filled with power, such as the Golden Fleece or the Girdle of Hippolyta, among other examples.

- Intelligence, deceit, and ingenuity (as shown in Odysseus) were other attributes that were revered by people. The mythical hero was not created just by his physical prowess.

Some people were able to get an endless afterlife by apotheosizing themselves as minor gods, while others were able to achieve perpetual recall through oral traditions.

Throughout the ages, revered historical figures have prompted the creation of devoted fan bases as well as memorials and shrines in their honor. This paid tribute to the influence they had.

Their failures, like as Heracles' descent into madness and Theseus' betrayal of Ariadne, demonstrated that even heroes were subject to human frailties that extended beyond mere mortality.

The basic Greek ideals of courage, loyalty, fate, compassion, and standing up for what is right in spite of the odds were underlined in their tales.

Famous Greek Heroes (Heracles, Perseus, Theseus etc.)

The epic of Greek mythology is filled to the brim with larger-than-life heroes, whose exploits of bravery, humor, and endurance never fail to enthrall audiences. This chapter provides an introduction to some of the most well-known Greek heroes, such as Heracles, Perseus, and Theseus, as well as a summary of their respective stories and an analysis of the lasting relevance of their exploits.

Heracles

Heracles, more often known by his Roman name Hercules, was the son of the deity Zeus and the human woman Alcmene. He is famously regarded as the most powerful of all mortal men and gods. His life was defined by a series of astonishing accomplishments, the most well-known of which are known as the Twelve Labors. Hera, the wife of Zeus, punished him by giving him a series of chores that seemed difficult to do as a sort of atonement for the fact that he had killed his wife and children when he was overcome with madness.

Heracles was able to complete his tasks by relying on a combination of his enormous strength, his ingenuity, and the occasional assistance of the gods. Some of the tasks he was tasked with completing include slaying terrifying beasts such as the Nemean Lion and the Hydra, as well as performing colossal feats such as cleaning the Augean stables in a single day and capturing Cerberus, the three-headed dog of the underworld.

Medusa was killed by Perseus, often known as "The Slayer."

Another one of Zeus's demigod sons, Perseus, is famed for killing Medusa, the Gorgon who had the power to transform men into stone just by looking at them. Perseus was born to a mortal woman named Dana, and his life was fraught with peril from the moment he was born. His own grandfather, King Acrisius, was afraid that a prophesy would come true and that his grandson would murder him.

Perseus was given several magical tools by the gods, such as sandals with wings, a hat that turned him invisible, a mirrored shield, and a sickle, so that he might vanquish Medusa. He was able to approach Medusa without being transformed to stone, behead her, and get away from her sisters all thanks to these items. The adventures of Perseus continued as he saved Princess Andromeda from a sea monster and unintentionally fulfilled the prophesy by murdering his grandpa. This allowed him to carry on with his exploits.

Theseus is known as the hero of Athens.

Theseus, the legendary king of Athens, is most remembered for traveling to Crete in order to slay the Minotaur, a monster with the body of a man and the head of a bull, who inhabited the labyrinth that had been constructed by Daedalus. Theseus offered to put an end to the Minotaur's demand for human sacrifices in order to pacify the monster.

Theseus successfully negotiated the labyrinth, killed the Minotaur, and then followed the thread back out of the maze, therefore rescuing himself and the other Athenians with whom he was traveling. Ariadne, the daughter of King Minos of Crete, had handed Theseus a ball of thread. After returning to Athens, Theseus transformed himself into a wise and just king and instituted a number of social and political changes.

Jason, in search of the fabled Golden Fleece

The most important event in Jason's life was guiding his fellow heroes, the Argonauts, on a treacherous journey to Colchis, which was located on the end of the known world, in order to collect the Golden Fleece. The voyage that Jason undertook was fraught with danger, from the conflict with harpies to the perilous passage through the Clashing Rocks.

Jason was successful in recovering the Golden Fleece and regaining his rightful position as King of Iancus with the assistance of the sorceress Medea, who developed romantic feelings for him during their time together. The fact that his connection with Medea resulted in tragedy, however, exemplifies the frequently contradictory and multifaceted nature of Greek heroes.

Odysseus, sometimes known as "The Mastermind Behind the Trojan War,"

In Greek mythology, Odysseus is a significant person who is recognized for his intelligence, eloquence, and ingenuity. He was the king of Ithaca.

The epic poem "The Odyssey," written by Homer, tells the story of the hero's return home after the Trojan War, which takes place over a period of 10 years.

Odysseus was one of the most important figures in the Trojan War. He is credited with coming up with the plan for the Trojan Horse, which ultimately resulted in the destruction of the city of Troy. His trip return to Ithaca was fraught with peril and difficulty at every turn, involving run-ins with the Lotus-Eaters, the Cyclops Polyphemus, the witch-goddess Circe, and the lethal Sirens, to name just a few of his adversaries along the way.

The Greek idea of "Metis," which may be translated as "skillful cunning," is shown by Odysseus's use of cunning and tenacity during the whole journey. His exploits shed light on the overarching concept of the hero's journey, which is a pattern of story structure that has inspired the telling of tales in a wide variety of cultures and time periods.

Achilles was widely regarded as the most capable fighter during the Trojan War.

According to Homer's "Iliad," the story of the Trojan War, Achilles is widely considered to have been the greatest warrior that ever lived. Achilles, the son of the mortal Peleus and the sea goddess Thetis, was rumored to have superhuman strength and invulnerability, with the exception of his heel.
The narrative of Achilles is driven primarily by the emotions of honor, pride, and fury. The anger that he displays against Agamemnon, who is in charge of the Greek army, and the following departure that he makes from the fight have devastating effects on the Greeks. Achilles does not return to the battle until after his close friend Patroclus has been put to death by Hector, the ruler of the Trojans.

Achilles' subsequent fury and sadness motivate him to murder Hector, disgrace the body, and finally return it to King Priam in a moving demonstration of shared humanity despite the horrors of war. This occurs after Achilles learns that Hector has been killed. Although it is not detailed in the Iliad, Achilles is said to have been killed by a bullet to the heel fired by Paris, who was Hector's brother. This is a well-known aspect of the myth surrounding Achilles.

The one and only Bellerophon, the Master of Pegasus

The tale of the hero Bellerophon is one that is filled with both remarkable victories and heartbreaking defeats. His most famous accomplishments include taming the winged horse Pegasus and killing the Chimera, a terrible beast that had the body of a lion, the tail of a serpent, and the head of a goat.

The arrogance that led Bellerophon to believe he could fly Pegasus all the way up to Mount Olympus, the home of the gods, was the cause of his demise. This act of arrogance displeased the gods, and as a result, they forced him to fall and cause him to spend out the rest of his life in agony while being ostracized by everyone.

Orpheus was known as "The Musician Who Charmed All"

Orpheus was a mythological figure in ancient Greek religion who was a musician, poet, and prophet. He was noted for his ability to use music to enchant not just living creatures but inanimate objects as well. In one of the most heartbreaking love stories from Greek mythology, he plays a pivotal role as a character.

Orpheus traveled to the Underworld after the death of his wife Eurydice, who had been killed by a snake bite. He hoped to bring her back from the dead. The gods of the underworld, Hades and Persephone, were moved to compassion by his song, and they consented to free Eurydice on the condition that Orpheus refrain from looking back at her until they reached the surface. Tragically, Orpheus did glance back, which led to Eurydice being sent back to the Underworld where she would remain there forever.

Not only do the exploits of these heroes make for exciting storytelling, but they also serve as reflections of the values, worries, and aspirations of ancient Greek society. They struggle with concepts such as honor, pride, love, and loss, in addition to the complicated dynamic that exists between gods and mortals. Each hero offers a distinct perspective from which to investigate the complex web of Greek mythology and the ongoing influence that it has had on the collective cultural imagination. This is true regardless of whether the hero's strengths lie in their physical or intellectual abilities. The heroic figures of Greek mythology are more than just fictional people from the past. They are representative of a wide range of facets of the human experience, including resiliency, inventiveness, ambition, and arrogance. Their stories address timeless topics like honor, bravery, love, and the quest for greatness, which makes them accessible and interesting to readers and viewers from many eras and countries.

These heroes are more than just cultural icons; they also function as personifications of particular ideas. Heracles, who possessed enormous strength, is a symbol of both the physical power and the enduring resilience that it takes to succeed. Perseus is the epitome of cunning and ingenuity, as he uses his brains to triumph over obstacles that at first appear to be insurmountable. Theseus, as an enlightened monarch, serves as a model for leadership and civic duty. In his search for the Golden Fleece, Jason is a metaphor for the spirit of adventure and the perseverance required to pursue a noble goal in the presence of formidable challenges.

The Roman perspective on these Greek heroes is an intriguing cultural component to take into consideration. The Romans appropriated and retold the tales of these heroes in much the same way as they did the myths of the Greek gods. Heracles evolved into the legendary figure of Hercules over time, being synonymous with bravery and tenacity. The majority of Perseus' tale was preserved, including the part when he killed Medusa. However, Theseus did not play a prominent role in Roman mythology, which may have been due to the fact that he had such a strong relationship with the city-state of Athens.

Demigods and Other Mortals Who Became Legends

Despite the fact that heroes were venerated for their superhuman acts, some persons came to mythological stature not just due to their pedigree but also due to their brains, skills, or luck. Ancient Greek stories contained a wide variety of mortals who played a significant role in shaping history by their deeds and endeavors, in addition to the demigods who were the offspring of immortals.

Odysseus was able to prove that knowledge and cunning might be as effective as brute strength by outwitting the cyclops Polyphemus and navigating his way back to his kingdom in Ithaca via years of wandering in the desert. Other illustrious tacticians included renowned intellectuals like as Socrates as well as philosophers whose insights continue to educate people even in modern times.

Renown of an everlasting nature was also attained by legendary artists. Daedalus, the architect, designed the Labyrinth to trap the Minotaur. However, Icarus' unsuccessful attempt to fly demonstrates how innovations can have unexpected effects. Orpheus was able to mesmerize nature with his ethereal lyre, and by playing melodies, he was able to achieve even a temporary resuscitation of his lost love. This demonstrates the power that music has over life and death.

Serendipity was also responsible for the rise to stardom of some really ordinary people. It's possible that the Sybil who gave Aeneas her oracular prophecies and led him into Hades was actually an unknown priestess who was pulled out of obscurity by chance. And King Midas demonstrated that everyone, regardless of their background or station in life, is capable of acquiring even the most sought of prizes; yet, this does not come without a price.

The fact that legends may be built from the exploits of mere mortals whose brains, abilities, and luck carried them to remarkable places was demonstrated by the adaptability of these stories that went beyond demigods. Their permanent imprints serve as a reminder to us that even the most ordinary person have the capacity to achieve legendary accomplishments and influence the course of history, provided that they possess an extraordinary character, visionary abilities, or simply the favor of Fortune.

Additional information on some of the mortal characters who attained legendary status in Greek mythology is provided below:
Archers such as Philoctetes and the Amazons displayed technical prowess on a level beyond that of a normal human being.

Empedocles and other ancient Greek philosophers believed they were demi-gods who could exert power over the forces of nature.

Archimedes, whose inventiveness with mechanics and mathematics goes on even today, was one of the inventors who came after Daedalus.

Because their treatments were so effective, physicians like Asclepius were eventually elevated to the status of healing deities.

Hesiod, Orpheus, and Homer were among the poets and singers who were responsible for the composition of the thematically complex works that immortalized epic narratives.

Generals like as Brasidas and Leonidas inspired others via their bravery in battle, confronting death with dignity despite the impossibility of the odds.

Athletes who competed in the Olympic games, such as Milo of Croton, were famous for doing athletic feats of an inhuman level of strength, stamina, and ability.

Beautiful humans like Semele, Ganymede, and Cassandra were even able to arouse the sexual affections of the gods, which resulted in significant changes in their lives.

Politicians such as Lycurgus contributed to the formation of the mythical martial society of Sparta by enacting changes that were subsequently attributed to divine inspiration.

Their greater-than-life achievements in a variety of professions, whether they were the result of genius, luck, or the favor of a divine being, showed the finest of mortal potential and its hope for apotheosis via skill, character, and contributions to cultural recall.

Chapter 4: Significant Myths and Legends

Myths of Creation and the Cosmos

The beginning of Greek mythology coincides with the beginning of the world itself. These ancient tales, which are deep in wonder and symbolism, describe a universe that was formed from Chaos, an entity that is formless and void-like. The earliest divine entities, Gaia (the Earth), Tartarus (the Underworld), and Eros (Love), arose from the chaos that existed before. This first world was a harsh place, with the earth, the skies, and the sea all being in their unformed states as they awaited the advent of the Titans and the activities of the Olympian gods who would mold them.

Gaia and Uranus, her son and spouse, are the parents of the Titans in this heavenly family tree. Uranus is also known as "the Sky." These were the enormous and strong older gods that ruled over mankind throughout the Golden Age of human history. Uranus was dethroned by the Titans under the leadership of Cronus, who craved more power, and they used this victory to gain control of the universe. Cronus, who was worried about the prophecies that predicted his own destruction, ate his offspring in their entirety to prevent them from succeeding him as king. However, Cronus's wife Rhea prevented the death of their youngest child, Zeus, by substituting a stone wrapped in linen for the child's meal. Zeus, once he had reached adulthood, confronted and ultimately overcame Cronus, which resulted in the release of Zeus' siblings and the beginning of the rule of the Olympians.

As a result, Zeus, Poseidon, and Hades, the three brothers who emerged victors, were given equal shares of the universe. Hades was the ruler of the underworld, whereas Zeus was in charge of the sky and the sea. This hierarchical structure and the areas of influence of these primary gods are both established by the partition of the universe that is a key topic in Greek mythology. The epic poems attributed to Homer, the Iliad and the Odyssey, make frequent references to these kingdoms. By doing so, they emphasize the power that the gods wield inside their domains and the severe consequences that are in store for humans who disobey them.

The ancient Greeks believed that the universe was more than just a physical realm; rather, it was a complex network of relationships between the divine and the mortal worlds. Every aspect of the cosmos was assigned a god or goddess, beginning with Helios, the god of the sun, who traversed the sky on his chariot every day, and ending with Selene, the goddess of the moon, who did the same thing every night. Even impersonal ideas like victory (personified as Nike), love (personified as Eros), and time (personified as Chronos) were given human characteristics.

In Greek mythology, the stars and the patterns in the sky known as constellations each had their own unique importance. The whims and caprices of various gods were often responsible for giving several constellations their names after people from mythology. For instance, the myth of Callisto, a nymph who was turned into a bear by the envious Hera and who was subsequently put among the stars by Zeus, explains the origin of the Ursa Major constellation. Callisto was the daughter of Uranus and Pleione. In a similar manner, Orion, a well-known hunter, was granted a position in the universe after his death. However, he will spend eternity being followed across the sky by Scorpius, a scorpion that Gaia has dispatched to kill him.

In all of its splendor, the creation myth also serves as a metaphor of the ancient Greeks' efforts to comprehend the world in which they lived. The humanization of intangible concepts and components of nature served as a strategy for simplifying complex concepts related to the cosmos. They did this by giving the wind a name (Aeolus) and attributing the shifting of the seasons to the movements of a goddess (Persephone), both of which were attempts to bring order to what appeared to be the chaotic workings of nature.

It is interesting to note that in Greek mythology, the universe was not an unchanging thing. It was continuously transformed by divine quarrels, heroic journeys, and terrible catastrophes that took place throughout history. It was stated that the Trojan War generated an unimaginable amount of turmoil in both the mortal world and the heavenly realm. This event is considered to be one of the most renowned in all of Greek mythology.

We are able to have a better appreciation for the richness and complexity of Greek mythology as a result of this investigation of creation myths and the universe. The Greeks' perception of the universe and the human condition, their fears and hopes, their curiosity and their wisdom are all reflected in these accounts. As we dive further into these narratives, we unearth not just the foundations of Western civilization, but also ageless legends that continue to reverberate with us in the modern day.

The ancient Greeks had a notion that was commonly referred to as "moira," which may also be rendered as "fate" or "destiny." It was not believed that the cosmos was disordered or chaotic, but rather orderly and predictable, as it was thought to be regulated by cosmic rules. This order was symbolized by the three Fate, also known as the Moirai: Clotho (Spinner), Lachesis (Allotter), and Atropos (Inevitable). Clotho was responsible for spinning the thread of life, while Lachesis measured it, and Atropos cut it off. These gods emphasized the Greeks' belief in a predetermined life destiny and highlighted the interdependence of human existence and the universe in general.

In addition to this, the ancient Greek way of life and decision-making was heavily influenced by the cosmos. The omens that were drawn from natural occurrences, such as thunderbolts from Zeus or the flights of birds, were considered as being messages from the gods. In addition, the stars were utilized not just for navigational purposes but also for divination, with the ascent and descent of particular constellations being interpreted as harbingers of future events.

In Greek mythology, there was a lot of back and forth between the heavenly and mortal realms, with gods intervening in human matters and heroes battling the gods. The ancient Greeks thought that the key to financial success was to strike a healthy balance between hubris, which may be defined as an excessive pride or self-confidence, and respect toward the gods. Icarus, who flew too near to the sun, and Niobe, who boasted that she was superior to the goddess Leto, both met their ends as a result of their defiance of the gods. This lesson may be learned from their stories. On the other hand, practicing religious devotion might result in heavenly favor being bestowed upon one; as was the case with the elderly couple Baucis and Philemon, who were honored by Zeus and Hermes for the hospitality they extended to guests.

The cultural practices and socioeconomic standards of ancient Greece were inextricably intertwined with the Greek universe. For instance, Zeus Xenias, the god who was considered to be the guardian of travelers, was in charge of the guest-friendship institution known as xenia. A breach of xenia was considered to be a grave transgression that may result in divine punishment. Arete, the goddess, was also considered to be the personification of the notion of arete, which means excellence. The pursuit of excellence in a variety of domains, including athletics, eloquence, and combat, was a central preoccupation in Greek civilization.

In its most fundamental sense, the Greek cosmos was not an immaterial substance but rather a component of the Greek worldview that was alive and actively breathing. It was entwined with every aspect of existence, from conception to demise, from human deeds to natural occurrences, and all in between. The rich cultural and intellectual environment of ancient Greece is evidenced by this dense network of linkages between the human world, the cosmos, and the divine. The universe was not only a backdrop for the divine drama, but also a participant in the process of life and myth being woven together, as well as a witness to it.

Myths About the Olympian Gods

The Olympian gods are the most important deities in Greek mythology. They are a fascinating cast of larger-than-life personalities, each of whom personifies a distinct facet of the human experience and the natural world. Their stories are woven into a complex tapestry of myths that tell much about the ancient Greeks' beliefs of deity, morality, nature, and mankind. These myths are weaved from the stories of the ancient Greeks.

Zeus is known as "the Ruler of the Gods."

Zeus was adored as the monarch of the gods, and it was believed that he ruled from his seat atop Mount Olympus. He was also known as the "Father of Gods and men." His authority was tested on more than one occasion, but the cunning and strength he personified with his thunderbolt served to secure his position as ruler. In the stories that surround Zeus, he is frequently portrayed as having a multitude of affairs with beautiful women and as being the ultimate arbiter of justice.

Hera is known as the Queen of the Gods.

Hera was the goddess of marriage, women, and childbirth in addition to being Zeus's wife and sister. Hera was also the queen of the gods. Myths about Hera frequently center on her vindictive attitude, notably toward Zeus's lovers and their children. Hera's vengeance is especially directed on Hera. However, she was also admired for the way that she defended marriage and the duties that women play within it.

Poseidon, often known as "The Earth-Shaker,"

Poseidon, who was the god of the sea as well as earthquakes and horses, had a great deal of authority. His trident had the ability to cause horrific earthquakes and enormous seas. Poseidon competed with Athena for the position of patronage in the city of Athens. He hit a rock, which resulted in the formation of a spring; however, Athena planted an olive tree, which was regarded as a more important present and earned her the adoration of the city.

Athena is a Greek goddess associated with both wisdom and battle.

Athena was the Greek goddess of learning, battle, and craftsmanship. She was said to have been born fully armed from Zeus' brow. In spite of the fact that she was a war Goddess, she was known more for being the goddess of strategic battle than of brutal conflict. Athena is shown as providing assistance to mythical heroes, such as Odysseus, and teaching humanity how to engage in productive activities.

Ares, often known as the God of War

Ares, as opposed to Athena, was the personification of the bloody and cruel aspects of battle. He was not well liked by either the gods or the mortals, and he only had a few temples devoted to him. In his legends, he is frequently shown to be in uncomfortable or otherwise compromised circumstances, which serves to further emphasize his unfavorable standing.

Aphrodite.

Aphrodite was the Greek goddess of love, beauty, and sexual desire. She was created from the froth of the sea. Her tales frequently contain romantic entanglements and conflicts, which is appropriate given that love is a force that can be powerful and occasionally chaotic. One of the most well-known stories about her centers on the prince of Troy, Paris, who is said to have given Aphrodite the golden apple of strife as a gift, thereby paving the way for the Trojan War.

Hermes was known as "the Messenger of the Gods"

Hermes was the god of thieves, merchants, and language as well as travel and trade. He was the gods' messenger, and with the assistance of his winged sandals, he was able to relay Zeus's commands to the gods as quickly as possible. Hermes was also renowned for his shrewdness, as is seen in the stories that tell of his stealing livestock from Apollo.

Hephaestus is known as the "Blacksmith of the Gods."

Hephaestus, the Greek deity of fire and blacksmithing, was venerated for the quality of his work. In spite of the fact that he suffered from a physical disability, he was highly esteemed among the Olympians due to his talent for fashioning things that were both beautiful and potent, including the weapons that were used by the gods.

Apollo and Artemis

Apollo and Artemis, the twin children of Zeus and Leto, were connected to a diverse array of spheres throughout Greek mythology. As the deity of the sun, music, and prophecy, Apollo was revered by the Ancient Greeks as a shining example of order and harmony. Artemis, the Greek goddess of the moon, virginity, and hunting, defended both women and the wild places they called home.

Demeter and Persephone

The Eleusinian Mysteries were a set of mysterious ceremonies that promised a good afterlife. At the center of these mysteries were the goddess Demeter, who was responsible for agriculture, and her daughter Persephone, who was connected with spring and the underworld. The changing of the seasons is explained by their story, in which the goddess Persephone is kidnapped by Hades but is eventually permitted to return for part of the year.

The ancient Greek worldview may be understood via the lens of these tales, which are as different as they are interesting. In spite of their supernatural position, the Olympians are shown to have human feelings and imperfections, which helps humans connect with them on a deeper level. By gaining a comprehension of these tales, we obtain a fuller appreciation of the lasting effect that Greek mythology has had.

When we go deeper into the stories that surround the Olympian gods, we discover a rich mixture of drama, wisdom, and moral precepts that continue to connect with people in our times. Because each god and goddess has their own distinct personality and backstory, they each illustrate a particular aspect of the human condition and the experiences that are shared by all people.

Dionysus was worshiped as the god of ecstasy and wine.

Dionysus, the only Olympian to have a father who was a mortal, was the god of wine, pleasure, and celebration. He was also known as Bacchus. Because of his dual personality, he embodied both the euphoria and the destructive possibilities of drunkenness. The importance of the theater in Dionysian rites might be interpreted as a reflection of the deity Dionysus's impact on drama and performance.

Hestia is known as the Goddess of the Home and Hearth.

Hestia was the sister of Zeus and was worshiped as the goddess of the home, the hearth, and domestic life. She did not have any exciting experiences as her siblings had. Instead, she made sure that the home of the gods was always calm, which was a metaphor of the solace and shelter that the home afforded. Her involvement in public life was similarly significant, as evidenced by the fact that the hearth in a city's Prytanea (also known as a town hall) was named after her in order to honor the communal spirit of the populace.

The connections that exist between the divine beings

The Olympians did not exist in a vacuum as figures. Their complicated connections, including their alliances, rivalries, love affairs, and familial ties, contributed further levels of complexity to their mythology. For example, Aphrodite and Hephaestus were married; yet, Aphrodite's many relationships, most famously with Ares, gave suspense to their story. Another reoccurring idea was the fierce competition that existed between the gods Athena and Poseidon.

The battle between gods and mortals

The Olympians engaged in regular interaction with mortals, which usually resulted in conflict or the genesis of heroes. Heracles and Perseus were only two of the countless mortal heroes who could trace their lineage back to Zeus. These demi-gods, or heroes, were frequently challenged by the fact that they had a dual legacy, which required them to either carry out heroic feats, endure the wrath of their divine father, or seek reconciliation with their divine parent.

The Presence of the Gods in Daily Life

The influence of the Olympians extended beyond the realm of epic stories and into many aspects of daily life. Each city had its own patron deity, whose blessing was sought in order to ensure the city's continued success. In their honor, celebrations took place all throughout the world, including the Dionysia in Athens and the Olympic Games in Olympia. Seafarers would pray to Poseidon for a risk-free journey, soldiers would call upon Ares or Athena for success, and newlyweds would make sacrifices to Hera in the hopes of having a happy union.

The importance of interpretation and influence

The gods and the mythology surrounding them have been interpreted in a variety of different ways throughout history, with these readings reflecting shifting cultural, intellectual, and artistic currents. For instance, the Romans identified the Olympians with their gods, which resulted in a merging of the attributes and stories associated with each group. During the Renaissance period, depictions of Greek gods that served as emblems of humanistic values appeared in works of art and literature.

The Olympian gods, with their vivid personalities and enthralling tales, provide a glimpse into the religious and cultural lives of the ancient Greeks by providing a window into their mythology. Their stories delve into ageless topics like power, love, fury, and wisdom, all of which continue to pique our interest. As we uncover more of these tales, we not only find the fantastic, but also the deeply human aspects of the characters.

The Trojan War and Homer's Epics

The Trojan War, the most memorable epic war associated with the Greek culture, came to be defined by two massive literary masterpieces. Homer, a poet who was blind, wrote sweeping epics called the Iliad and the Odyssey in which he immortalized the narrative for all time with his fascinating and beautiful lines. These foundational poems had an indelible impact on the literary legacy of the West.

The focus of the epic poem "The Iliad" was on a crucial phase of the conflict that lasted for a decade. More particularly, it was on Achilles' anger at Agamemnon, which led to his removing his troops' protection. Emotionally engaging portrayals of the Achaeans and Trojans, which explore their humanity despite their extraordinary fighting skill, are weaved among gripping tales of martial prowess and devastating battle scenes between the two sides.

The story of The Odyssey then follows the valiant adventure of Odysseus, who is cunning and clever, as he makes his way back to Ithaca after enduring incredible trials and escaping the disdain of Poseidon. His ingenuity and unwavering allegiance emphasized Greek principles of intellectual cunning combined with tenacity of spirit. These attributes cemented his standing as a prototype for conducting oneself decently despite the unpredictability of life.

Characters with depth and personality came to life in these poems written by Homer, who was a lyrical narrative method master. These poems have been read and reread for more than two millennia. Their legendary story was crucial in laying the groundwork for the later Western epic genre. Its resonant universal themes investigated human nature, fate and free choice, as well as mankind's interaction with divinities that were not always predictable. Homer's poetry compositions assured that the legendary Trojan War and its lasting ramifications would forever penetrate Greek cultural memory, despite the fact that the historicity of the event remains dubious.

The conclusion of the Trojan War and its repercussions:

After many years of battle that reached a stalemate, the Greeks finally came up with the idea for the infamous Trojan Horse hoax that was conceived by Odysseus.

They gave the impression that they were sailing away, but in reality, they secreted elite soldiers inside the enormous wooden horse and left it as a sacrifice.

Because the Trojans thought they had triumphed, they brought the horse inside the gates of their city to keep as a prize. At some point during the night, Greek soldiers made their way outside and unlocked the city gates.

The Greeks surprised the Trojans and launched an attack on the city of Troy, which resulted in the destruction of the city. King Priam and a great number of other Trojans perished.

Aeneas, who would later go on to create Rome and is mentioned in Virgil's Aeneid, was one of the few important Trojans who managed to flee.

The voyage back home was fraught with danger for the triumphant Greeks, and many of them were never seen again. Odysseus was tested over the course of many years. Agamemnon was killed in this incident.

A dark period descended over the area as a result of the battle, which was responsible for the destruction of the thriving civilizations of the Mycenaeans and the Trojans. The collapse of these nations made space for the establishment of new Greek states such as Athens and Sparta.

Therefore, while they were successful in accomplishing their goal, the protracted battle exacted a tremendous cost and drastically affected the political and cultural environment of the globe around the Aegean.

Additional information on Homer's epics and the mythology surrounding the Trojan War:

There were many different accounts of the conflict, but most historians agree that it took place in the late Bronze Age, circa 1200 BCE. Academics disagree over whether or not it actually occurred.

The fight started when Paris, a Trojan prince, made his choice between Aphrodite and Helen, the wife of Menelaus, King of Sparta. Paris ran away with Helen.

To exact their revenge, the Greeks formed an alliance under the leadership of King Agamemnon of Mycenae and sailed one thousand ships toward the city of Troy.

Other epic poets, like as Lesches and Arctans, contributed to the development of the mythos by writing their own cycle epics that covered different time periods of the conflict.

Odysseus is credited with coming up with the idea for the Trojan Horse ploy, which ultimately led to the Greeks breaking the deadlock and winning the battle.
The epics focus on Achilles' fury and Odysseus' trip home from the battle that lasted ten years, and they only retell a few weeks from the last year of the conflict.

Both poems emphasize the interference of gods in human affairs and the arbitrary nature of fate, especially when it comes to the lives of heroes who are brilliant and skilled.

Archaeology confirmed the locations of several of the places listed in the Homeric epics, including Troy, Mycenae, and Ithaca; this lent greater credence to the Homeric narratives.

Throughout the Greek-speaking world throughout the centuries that followed, the poems played a significant role in shaping cultural identity and education.

Myths of Adventure and Heroism

The anthology of stories that make up Greek mythology is replete with accounts of arduous journeys, brave heroes, and difficult tests. Not only did these tales provide entertainment, but they also functioned as a means of imparting moral and cultural teachings through illuminating principles like as valor, intelligence, dignity, and piety.

The Adventure of the Hero

The hero's journey is a narrative framework that can be found in many Greek myths. It consists of a summons to adventure, a risky trip, and a victorious return. The hero's journey typically involves a confrontation with heavenly forces, the completion of perilous missions, and the acquisition of a valuable prize.

Perseus, often known as "The Gorgon Slayer,"

The story of Perseus, who was the son of Zeus and Dana, is considered to be one of the oldest hero stories. Perseus decided to retrieve the head of Medusa, the Gorgon whose glance could turn humans to stone, so that his mother would not have to enter into a marriage that she did not desire. Perseus accomplished his mission with the help of magical objects bestowed to him by the gods. These things were Hermes' winged sandals and Athena's mirrored shield. He used Medusa's head to free his mother and, according to some versions of the myth, to build the city of Mycenae.

Theseus Confronts the Minotaur and Explores the Labyrinth

Theseus, the fabled king of Athens, is said to have embarked on yet another well-known expedition in his narrative. Theseus volunteered to go into the Labyrinth in order to put an end to the sacrifices that were being made to the Minotaur, a creature who had the body of a man but the head of a bull. Theseus was able to successfully explore the Labyrinth, slay the Minotaur, and guide his fellow Athenians to safety with the assistance of the charmed thread that Ariadne had given him.

Heracles: The Twelve Labors is the name of the play.

Heracles, one of the most famous Greek heroes, was required to do the Twelve Labors, a series of challenging activities, in order to make up for the murder of his wife and children, which he committed while under the influence of Hera's tyrannical influence and as a result of his insanity. His efforts, which included killing the Nemean Lion, capturing the Golden Hind of Artemis, and recovering Cerberus from the Underworld, gave him great acclaim and, finally, earned him a seat among the gods. His labors were rewarded with a place among the gods.

The Golden Fleece, also known as Jason

Another well-known heroic story is that of Jason and his search for the Golden Fleece. As the commander of the Argonauts, Jason was faced with a number of difficulties along their expedition. These included overcoming the sleepless dragon that was protecting the fleece and traversing the Clashing Rocks. In addition, the sorceress Medea, who would later become his wife, provided him with some magical help throughout his voyage.

The epic poem "Odysseus: The Journey Home"

Odysseus's trip home from the Trojan War, which takes place over the course of 10 years in Homer's Odyssey, is a story about cunning and perseverance. Odysseus's travels represent the hardships and resiliency of a hero seeking his home and identity. Faced with trials such as refusing the singing of the Sirens, evading the cyclops Polyphemus, and sailing between Scylla and Charybdis, Odysseus's experiences reflect the struggles and resiliency of a hero.

The Greatest Hero and the Most Holy Being

The connection that exists between the hero and the gods is a reoccurring motif in the tales that surround Greek heroes. Heroes are frequently demi-gods, which means that they were born of a mortal and a god, which positions them in a special position between the realms of the mortal and the divine. Due to their mixed ancestry, the gods frequently look favorably upon them but also test them. Hera constantly harassed Heracles, the son of Zeus, but he also got heavenly assistance in his labors. Heracles was the hero of the labors.

The Part That Women Play in Various Heroic Myths

Women have important roles in these myths, despite the fact that most of the protagonists in the stories are males. They might be a source of assistance or a challenge, a romantic interest or a wise counselor. Throughout the course of their adventures, heroes like Odysseus and Perseus frequently sought advice from Athena. A mortal lady named Ariadne was extremely helpful to Theseus throughout his journey. On the other hand, women may also provide challenges or be the cause of catastrophe, as seen by the Sirens in Homer's Odyssey and Medea in Jason's final years.

The intersection between heroism and mortality

Even though they sprang from supernatural bloodlines and possessed exceptional skills, Greek heroes were still human. The fact that they were mortal, in addition to the fact that they were heroes, made their actions more respectable and their personas more approachable. They were subject to the whole range of human emotions, were fallible, and were aware that their lives were finite. Achilles, the greatest Greek warrior during the Trojan War, made a decision that reflected the Greek ideal of a heroic life by opting for a short life filled with glory rather than a long life filled with insignificance.

What Our Greek Heroes Have Left Behind

The impact of Greek stories about heroes has been felt far beyond the boundaries of ancient Greece. Over the course of several centuries, these tales have been recounted and reinterpreted, exerting an influence not just on literature and the arts, but also on philosophy, and even psychology. The scholar Joseph Campbell is credited with being the first person to identify the notion of the "hero's journey," which has been employed in a broad variety of modern storytelling, from Star Wars to Harry Potter.

The foundations of Greek mythology are laid with these exciting and heroic tales, which are rife with peril, enchantment, and instructive life lessons. They are a reflection of the ancient Greeks' anxieties and ambitions, their ideas of honor and heroism, and their view of the universe and human nature.

The heroes, despite their exceptional qualities, are not without flaws. They are not perfect and often make blunders. Despite this, the Greeks were able to examine the intricacies of mankind via the heroes' weaknesses as well as the ways in which they responded to obstacles. It is important to note that even the gods, despite their immortality and strength, frequently played supporting roles to the human heroes, which highlights the relevance of human potential and resiliency. As we explore further into these tales, we not only come across exciting experiences, but also ageless truths about the nature of the human experience.

In addition, these myths continue to function as a wellspring of creative ideas and a tool for investigating aspects of human nature. The obstacles that the heroes had to overcome were metaphors for more general issues in life, and their bravery and resiliency provided inspiration and direction. They are forced to ponder on ethics and values as a result of the moral conundrums they face.

Not only do the heroic stories of ancient Greece contain exciting adventures, but they also contain profound and ageless narratives about mankind. These tales, which combine the human and the divine, as well as the everyday and the exceptional, take us on heroic adventures that need us to have bravery, make sacrifices, and learn more about ourselves. They serve as a constant reminder of the greatness that lies inside everyone of us, the significance of prudence and ingenuity, and the eternal force of the human spirit.

Tragic Myths of Love and Betrayal

Throughout the whole of Greek mythology, elaborate stories of love frequently carried with them ominous undercurrents of deceit, curses, and devastating betrayal that strongly connected with audiences. These tragic tales continue to have an influence on current storytellers due to the universal truths they contain, which was reflected in the plays written by famous tragedians like as Aeschylus, Sophocles, and Euripides.

One such myth that has stood the test of time is the story of the attractive Phaedra, who develops an illicit desire for her stepson Hippolytus. She lied about his having committed rape in order to avoid the humiliation of being rejected by him, and this act of slander ultimately led to the murder of the hunter-hero at the hands of a huge sea creature. In a similar manner, Deianeira's misdirected "love potion" for Hercules resulted in an inadvertent and terrible betrayal by Nessus the centaur, who was divinely cruel.

A particularly heartbreaking tragedy occurred when Princess Ariadne gave in to Theseus's advances and fell in love with him. Despite her assistance in his defeat of the Minotaur, Theseus cast her out on a desolate island once the battle was over. The desperation that the Cretan girl felt exemplified how love is susceptible to chance.

But even in the midst of suffering, the seeds of transformation can sprout. The dark female takeover of power from a patriarchal society may be seen in Medea's vindictive, passion-fueled sorcery that led to the destruction of Jason, her faithless husband, and their children along with him.

The ancient Greeks gained a greater grasp of love's complicated delights as well as the cruelties that may convert it into hatred via the use of legendary instances that were both cautionary and powerful in nature. Within these timeless lyrical figures, audiences continue to understand the murky truths of the precarious nature of relationships.

The following are some more examples of tragic love stories that appear in Greek mythology:

- Orpheus and Eurydice - Orpheus ventures into the underworld with his lyre in order to save his wife Eurydice, but he ends up losing her once more since he broke Hades' rule that said they couldn't look back as they were leaving.

- Hero and Leander were a couple who were in love despite the fact that they lived on opposite sides of the Hellespont. Every night, Leander would swim over to visit Hero, guiding himself with a lamp that she lit. However, there was one night when a storm caused him to drown in the process.

- Pyramus and Thisbe were two Babylonian lovers whose families disapproved of their intention to wed one other. They had planned to meet each other in secret beneath a mulberry tree, but due to a misunderstanding, each of them ended up thinking the other had passed away, which led to them taking their own lives.

- Troilus and Cressida - Princes of Troy and Greece who fall in love during the Trojan War; nevertheless, Cressida is subsequently traded for a Greek prisoner of war and betrays Troilus. - Cressida is later swapped for a Greek prisoner of war.

- Despite the fact that Achilles and Patroclus are described in the Iliad as being the closest of friends, their relationship is seen as romantic by certain academics. Achilles is motivated to get revenge on Patroclus for his death at Troy.

- Iphigenia is the name of Agamemnon's daughter, whom he is forced to offer as a sacrifice to the gods in order to secure favorable winds for the Trojan expedition, against the opposition of his wife Clytemnestra.

The Greeks lived in a harsh environment, and many of their sad stories reveal how love may be easily broken amidst the unpredictability and terrible turns of fate.

Chapter 5: Mythical Creatures and Monsters

Creatures of the Sea and Waterways

In Greek mythology, numerous habitats below the waves were inhabited by strange creatures that were well suited to their respective watery domains. The older sea deity Poseidon ruled over the aquatic regions, which were teeming with exotic species that might be both scary and fantastical.

Swimming among Poseidon's attendants were visiting goddesses like as the Nereids, who adorned the shorelines of the placid seas. Even more terrifying was the kraken Octopus Polyphemus, who blinded Odysseus with his gaze. Among the aquatic creatures was the multi-headed Lernaean Hydra, as well as the pit of Charybdis, which devoured fleets within its gullet. Merfolk species assumed forms that were half-human, such as the enticing music of the Sirens, which lured sailors to their deaths.

Under the watery realms, there lived Stymphalian man-eating birds and Lernaean hydra that took either a single form or a double form in terms of the races that differentiated humans and other creatures. On riverbanks, one may perhaps collect water nymphs such as Naiades within a tree or spring. Their appearance and disappearance matched the ebb and flow of the natural world.

This amplitude brought to light the ageless appeal of the oceans, which can be both terrifying and joyful, and it mirrored humanity's connection with enigmatic watery regions that are too big and quirky to fully comprehend or tame. Even if they did not exist in real life, Greek sea monsters served as a reminder of our common roots, which are still bound to the primitive rhythms and dangers of elemental waterways. Their legacy contributes to the enrichment of our contemporary imaginings in ways that go beyond what rational steel appears capable of showing.

The following is more information on legendary animals that lived in the seas and rivers of Greece:

- Monsters that tormented sailors in the Strait of Messina, known as Scylla and Charybdis, were a metaphor for the unpredictability of life at sea. They were located between Italy and Sicily.

- Nereids are shown as riding hippocampi (seahorses) in many artworks because they were graceful feminine sea nymphs who followed Poseidon and Thetis.

- Tritons are mermen that serve as messengers for Poseidon. Their upper torsos are human-like, and their bottom bodies are similar to dolphins'.

- Freshwater spirits that live in lakes and springs and have symmetrical bodies like water bulls or waterfowls are known as escheats.

- Potamic are river gods that appeared as bearded men and ruled over particular streams in ancient Japan.

- Phoebe and the Oceanids were guided across the skies by an enigmatic sea deity named Proteus, who was also capable of assuming other forms.

- Iconic creatures such as the Lernaean Hydra that live in bodies of water or mangroves are referred to as sea serpents.

- Nessus was a centaur that Hercules murdered as he was attempting to cross a river. Nessus's subsequent deceit led to fatal consequences.

Therefore, despite the fact that these figures were terrible, they also reflected the variety of nature and the endeavor that mythology made to comprehend aquatic environments that were still filled with mystery for the ancients.

In addition to the Nereids and the Tritons, Poseidon, the Greek god of the sea, was intimately linked with a number of different species of sea animals, including the following:

- Mythological animals known as hippocamps or hippocamps possessed the forelegs, neck, and head of a horse, while the rear half of their body was that of a fish.

- Dolphins were regarded sacred animals and were endowed with extraordinary abilities of prophecy. They were frequently pictured riding behind Poseidon's chariot.

- Poseidon, who was sometimes depicted riding a majestic sea horse, was said to have been the inventor of the first horse, and he was occasionally seen riding one.

- Mythical animals that had the top body of a goat and the bottom body of a fish, known as sea goats, were frequently used to move Poseidon's chariot.

- Physeter (whales): It was believed that Poseidon had a deep connection to the enormous whales and other sea beasts who possessed terrifying power.

- Crabs - Poseidon held these crustaceans in the highest regard, and in several stories, crabs were credited with possessing amazing abilities.

- Octopuses Clever and octopuses with eight arms, like as Polyphemus, symbolized Poseidon's sovereignty over the sea domain.

Poseidon's aquatic domain was home to a variety of seals, some of whom possessed the ability to predict the future while others simply enjoyed being playful.

Therefore, Poseidon reigned over a diverse menagerie of sea-related species, both real and legendary, that ranged from peaceful to menacing.

Dangerous Creatures and Killers

In Greek mythology, there is an abundance of terrible animals and killers, each one more dreadful than the one who came before them. These fearsome entities, who are frequently dispatched by the gods as punishments or tests, are a mainstay in the stories of heroes. They stand for both tangible dangers and metaphorical obstacles that must be surmounted.

Gorgons

The Gorgons were a terrible set of sisters who had hair made of live, poisonous snakes, hands made of metal, and sharp teeth. The most well-known of these monsters, Medusa, has the ability to transform anybody who gazed at her into stone. Perseus, the hero, was the one who brought about her demise. He employed a mirrored shield that had been granted to him by Athena in order to dodge her lethal stare and behead her.

The Minotaur

The Minotaur, a monster with the body of a man and the head of a bull, was the son of Queen Pasiphae of Crete and a magnificent bull. Legend has it that the Minotaur terrorized Crete for generations. The Minotaur was kept in the Labyrinth and fed an annual tribute of young Athenians until the hero Theseus was able to slay him with the assistance of Ariadne's thread.

The Hydra

The Hydra was a water-based snake that had several heads, each of which could be severed and replaced by two new heads. During the second labor that Heracles endured, he was able to vanquish this terrifying beast, which not only had lethal breath but also blood. Heracles ensured that the heads would not regenerate by cauterizing the necks of each individual when he severed it with his sword with the assistance of his nephew Iolaus.

The Sirens

The Sirens were mythical bird-women whose alluring and lovely songs led unsuspecting sailors to their deaths at sea. They are a metaphor for the perils of giving in to temptation and losing focus. Odysseus was able to avoid their lethal seduction in the Odyssey by having his men block their ears with wax and tying him to the ship's mast. This allowed him to hear their song without being affected by it.

Scylla and Charybdis

The sea monsters known as Scylla and Charybdis were said to be found in close proximity to one another and presented a twofold danger to ships that were sailing there. A monster known as Scylla, which had six heads on long necks, was known to kidnap sailors off their ships. The vortex known as Charybdis, which was located on the other coast, was known to consume entire ships. Odysseus was forced to choose between these two perils, and as a result, he suffered the loss of six of his men at the hands of Scylla.

The Sphinx

The Sphinx, a monster with the body of a lion, the wings of an eagle, and the face of a woman, tormented the people of Thebes with a perilous puzzle and killed anybody who was unable to solve it by strangling them to death. Oedipus, the hero of the story, was able to solve the puzzle and save the city by relying on his intellect rather than his physical power.

Cerberus, often known as the Hound of Hades

In Greek mythology, Cerberus is a recurrent figure. He is a hound with three heads that guards the gateway to the Underworld. Cerberus serves as a metaphor of the impenetrable barrier that separates the realm of the living from the world of the dead. Only a select few heroes, like as Heracles and Orpheus, were successful in outwitting Cerberus, typically by physical prowess or the allure of musical appeal.

The Lion of the Nemean Sea

During the first labor that Heracles went through, he was able to slay the Nemean Lion, an unbeatable beast that had golden fur and claws that were sharper than any mortal weapon. The hero made the astounding discovery that the lion's hide was impenetrable by any material, not even iron, bronze, or stone. Heracles eventually overcame the lion's resistance and managed to suffocate it. He then used the lion's hide as an impenetrable shield.

The Harpies are also known as the Snatchers.

Harpies were terrifying winged beings with the bodies of birds and the faces of women. They personified devastating wind gusts. Harpies were said to have faces similar to women. They were known for stealing objects and people, and when they were done, they frequently left a putrid odor in their wake. In the myth of Jason and the Argonauts, the Harpies are the villains that steal food from Phineus, the blind seer, on a consistent basis until the Boreades, the winged heroes, drive them away.

The Furies, also known as Vengeful Spirits

The Furies, also known as the Erinyes, were frightening deities associated with retribution. They punished mortals who took false oaths and committed horrific crimes, particularly those perpetrated against family members. Born from the blood of a castrated Uranus, they were responsible for their creation. Their dogged pursuit of justice brings to light the significance of loyalty to one's family and the truth in the society of ancient Greece.

These terrifying monsters provide a dimension of danger and excitement to Greek stories due to their lethal skills as well as their terrifying appearances. In spite of this, they do more than just add suspense to the narratives; rather, they serve a function. They are representations of many human anxieties, moral teachings, and natural occurrences, and they reflect abstract notions and society standards.

The effect of these creatures was not limited to the civilization of ancient Greece. You may find references to them in later Roman mythology, in literature from the Middle Ages and the Renaissance, and even in current books and movies. For instance, the Harpies afflict the souls of those who are envious in Dante's "Divine Comedy," and J.K. Rowling's "Fluffy," the three-headed hound in "Harry Potter and the Philosopher's Stone," is unmistakably based on Cerberus. Both of these creatures are derived from Greek mythology.

Furthermore, these legendary beasts continue to play important roles as symbols in today's society. The myth of the sirens, for example, is frequently employed as a metaphor for alluring but perilous temptations. The Sphinx is commonly connected with cryptic knowledge and conundrums, but the Furies represent unyielding justice.

Through the examination of these potentially lethal beings and murderers, we not only achieve a more profound comprehension of the mythology of ancient Greece but also obtain new insights into the common human experience. These ageless stories continue to enthrall, confound, and motivate us, which serves as a useful reminder of the power of storytelling as well as the everlasting appeal of the mythical realm. These terrible and interesting legendary monsters and killers play essential roles in Greek mythology. Greek mythology is filled with stories about them. They serve the purpose of putting the heroes' mettle to the test, typically depicting internal conflicts or external threats to society. The triumph of the hero against these monsters frequently represents the hero's triumph over fear, the transformation of chaos into order, or the acquisition of knowledge. The tales told about these fantastic beasts never fail to enthrall audiences, which is another evidence of the mythology of ancient Greece's continuing appeal.

These powerful animals also have a larger symbolic purpose, as they are meant to reflect a variety of facets that are associated with the human experience. It is possible to interpret the petrifying stare of the Gorgons as a representation of the paralyzing effects of terror. It's possible that the Minotaur, who was imprisoned in the Labyrinth, is a metaphor for the devastating power of our animalistic urges. The Sirens are a metaphor for the dangers of giving in to temptation, while Scylla and Charybdis represent the necessity of making challenging decisions. By vanquishing these beasts, the heroes of Greek mythology display the virtues of bravery, intelligence, and resiliency that have inspired countless generations throughout the ages.

Mythical Animals

In Greek mythology, humans were not the only inhabitants of the settings described; other, more fantastical creatures also lived there. In contrast to the unusual hybrid monsters that roamed free, farm animals carried significant symbolic importance.

Pasiphae saw visions of sacred bulls, which was the catalyst for Daedalus' cunning plan to get her pregnant with a Minotaur. The Golden-Fleeced Ram was successful in saving Phrixus and Helle, but it was the end of the adventure for Jason's Argonauts. Hercules was required to complete twelve labors, one of which was to kill the deadly Nemean Lion, which had teeth resembling arrowheads. Pegasi, winged horses, lifted Bellerophon until Pegasus, the leader of the Pegasi, flung him because he was getting too close to Mount Olympus.

The Centaur personified the conflicting parts of nature, acting as both a guide and an adversary during wedding ceremonies. Chiron was a wise figure who instructed Achilles and Jason in various healing techniques. Heracles and Bellerophon, respectively, were able to tame dangerous beasts like the nine-headed Lernaean Hydra and the man-eating Stymphalian Birds that were plaguing certain areas.

These depictions endowed ordinary cattle with a spiritual quality, whilst supernatural hybrids depicted the unfathomable depths of the forest that humans had difficulty grasping, confining, and developing. Even though they are fictitious, such tales aimed to impose human order on wild wildlife, representing the incomprehensible aspects of nature that would always escape the complete comprehension of humans. Their legacy serves as a reminder that tales may originate from realities in the same way that realities can originate from imaginations.

The ancient Greeks imagined that there were limitations to their ability to subdue the wild by populating untamed areas and oceans with monsters in an effort to compete with the total dominance of humans. Their animals embodied the vastness and mystique of the natural world, perpetually invoking feelings of reverence and terror in the same way that the living wilderness still does today, despite all attempts to domesticate it.

The following is more information on the mythological animals of Greek mythology:

- The Sphinx, a beast with the head of a woman that tormented Thebes with enigmas until Oedipus was able to vanquish it. posed questions that could not be answered by current knowledge.

- The Caledonians Boar is a monstrous wild boar that may be found in the Caledonian Forest and is pursued by heroes like Meleager. Frequently portrayed as wreaking havoc on the countryside.

- The terrifying three-headed dog known as Cerberus served as a gatekeeper at the entrance to Hades' domain in the underworld. representations of hellhounds with a lot of inspiration.

- Stymphalian Birds, Carnivorous man-eating birds with metallic feathers that they were able to fire as missiles and that terrified a city in Arcadian territory.

- The Chimera is a hybrid creature who sprang from Lycia and was slain by Bellerophon. It had the head of a goat, the body of a serpent, and the mane of a lion.
- Geryon - A three-bodied giant with red hair and bronzed skin who possessed cattle that were guarded by the two-headed dog Orthros. - Geryon was known for his fiery hair and bronzed complexion.

- Hercules was given the duty of taming the wild, man-eating horses belonging to the Bostonian monarch, the Mares of Diomedes. This was one of Hercules' heroic feats.

- Heracles slew the multi-headed sea monster known as Hydra in the lake of Mars. When one of its heads was severed, several appeared in its place.

- The Gorgons, these winged daemons have snakes for hair, and they have the ability to turn anybody who gazes at them into stone. Medusa is the most well-known of the Gorgons.

- The Geryon was a large three-headed giant with red hair and bronze complexion who lived on the island of Erythema and watched over a treasured herd of cattle. He was known for his fierce protection of the animals.

- Typhon was an enormous creature that was said to have one hundred dragon heads and fire flowing out of its mouth. It was portrayed as the final offspring of Gaia, but Zeus managed to vanquish it.

- The man-bull spawn of Pasiphae that was confined in the Labyrinth and fed on young men and boys that were brought to it as sacrifices is known as the Minotaur.

- Echidna is a mythical creature who is half-woman and half-serpent and is said to have mated with many monstrous beings, giving birth to creatures such as the Chimera, Cerberus, and Hydra.

- Giants are the gigantic Titans, such as Atlas, who dared to climb Mount Olympus in an effort to compete with the gods for their authority.

- Harpies are winged humanoid vultures with wings that have been known to steal food or abduct humans. They are a representation of harmful nature spirits.

- Scylla was a sea monster with several heads that was said to have lived in a sea cave opposite the whirlpool Charybdis and preyed on unsuspecting sailors.
Therefore, mythological beasts were utilized as a metaphor of the fury of nature as well as scary unknowns that posed a threat to people. Mythical monsters thereby personified enigmas that are beyond human explanation while also expressing humanity's existence amongst untamed wildness and serving as a mirror for its place in the natural world.

Hybrids and Monsters

Monsters and hybrid beings have a significant role to play in the expansive universe of Greek mythology. These creatures, which frequently contain aspects of both human and animal life, exemplify the ancient people's terror of and fascination with the unknown while also serving as symbols of chaos, peril, or ethical precepts. Their interactions with heroes function as tests, giving the heroes an opportunity to display their bravery, cleverness, or other admirable qualities.

Centaurs

One of the most well-known examples of a hybrid species is the centaur, which possesses the upper body of a person and the bottom body of a horse. They were noted for their wild and uncivilized conduct, which served as a metaphor for the elements of nature that cannot be controlled. One notable exception to this rule was Chiron, a smart and upright centaur who served as a mentor to a number of legendary Greek figures, including Achilles and Jason.

Satyrs

Satyrs were worshipers of Dionysus, the deity of wine and celebration, and were described as being half-human and half-goat. They personify the wild and untamed qualities of nature in all their glory. In Greek art, they were frequently shown as being lusty, inebriated, and cheerful animals.

Chimera

The Chimera, a monster that had the body of a lion, the tail of a snake, and the head of a goat projecting from its back, was a representation of things that appeared to be impossible but could actually be accomplished. It was defeated by Bellerophon, who rode the winged horse Pegasus, illustrating that one may triumph over fear with bravery and the assistance of divine intervention.

Minotaur

The Minotaur, a monster with the body of a man and the head of a bull, was the son of Queen Pasipha of Crete and a magnificent bull. Legend has it that the Minotaur terrorized Crete for generations. This monster, who was trapped in the Labyrinth, ate the young men who were sent from Athens as a form of tribute until the hero Theseus slew it.

Scylla

Scylla was a monster sea nymph that had been changed into a creature with six dog heads wrapped around her waist. Each dog head had a long neck and a row of vicious fangs. Scylla was a member of the Order of the Six-Headed Dog. Her metamorphosis, which is typically attributed to the witchcraft of Circe, is a commentary on the concepts of envy and retribution.

Typhon and Echidna

Typhon and Echidna, who are sometimes referred to as the father and mother of all monsters, are responsible for the birth of a great number of terrifying creatures. These monstrous offspring include the Chimera, the Hydra, and the Sphinx. Typhon, a behemoth with serpents for legs, fought Zeus for dominion but ultimately lost and was buried beneath Mount Etna after being vanquished.

Sirens

The bird-women known as the Sirens were famous for their entrancing vocals, which they used to entice sailors to their deaths with their songs. They are the personification of the peril posed by temptation as well as the terrible pull of the unknown. In Homer's Odyssey, Odysseus gives his troops the instruction to block their ears with beeswax so that they can withstand the sirens' music. This serves as a metaphor for the significance of avoiding giving in to harmful temptations.

Cyclopes

Cyclopes were giants with just one eye who were renowned for their strength and expertise in metalworking. The most well-known of them all was Polyphemus, who Odysseus eventually managed to blind. In contrast to the intelligence and skill displayed by heroes such as Odysseus, the Cyclops stand for all that is unsophisticated and backwards.

Griffin

The Griffin, a mythical monster with the body of a lion and the head and wings of an eagle, was seen as a protector of priceless relics and a representation of the omnipotence of a higher force. The image of a griffin has lasted through the years in a variety of guises, beginning with its frequent appearance in the artwork of ancient Greece.

The Hippocampal Formation

Poseidon, the Greek god of the sea, was said to be closely linked with the hippocampus, a mythical marine monster that had the upper body of a horse and the bottom body of a fish. This beast, which is frequently shown hauling the chariot of Poseidon, exemplifies the power and mystique of the ocean.

Harpies

Harpies were viewed as punitive spirits that tortured wrongdoers and grabbed people and goods. These bird-women were famed for their speed and their keen claws. Their name, which comes from the Greek word for "snatchers," alludes to the unexpected vanishing of items or persons.

These monsters, along with a number of other hybrids and monsters that appear in Greek mythology, act as metaphors for the fears, problems, and ambitions of humankind. In the stories of heroes and gods, they play pivotal roles, personifying natural forces, moral precepts, and societal standards.

In addition to the symbolic connotations that are associated with them, the ancient Greeks' conception of the universe may be inferred from these animals. They are a representation of the ancient people's desire to give the enigmas of nature, the difficulties of being human, and the whims of the gods a personality so that they may be understood and explained.

Additionally, the literary and artistic worlds have been profoundly altered as a result of the hybrids and monsters. They have been the source of inspiration for a myriad of adaptations and reinterpretations throughout the course of the ages, ranging from paintings from the Renaissance to current fantasy novels and films. These ageless beings, with their mix of human and animal characteristics, have the ability to continue to enthrall us with their mystique, symbolism, and story-telling prowess.

Last but not least, the everlasting attractiveness of these animals is illustrative of the human race's age-old preoccupation with the unusual and the unknown. They jolt us back to our most basic anxieties, the battles we've fought against hardship, and our never-ending need for knowledge and comprehension. As we proceed in our investigation of these fantastic beings, not only do we dig more into the intricate web of Greek mythology, but we also begin a more in-depth investigation into the nature of the human experience. These monstrous hybrids and creatures, who are just as interesting as they are dangerous, play important roles in Greek mythology. They reflect many facets of the human condition and the natural world, and they are a symbol of the ancient Greeks' quest to understand and personify the world around them.

It is frequently symbolic of the conflict between order and chaos, civilization and the wilderness, or virtue and vice that these meetings between these creatures and the heroes serve as trials or hurdles that need to be conquered. The vanquishing of these beasts is frequently interpreted as a symbol of the triumph of human intelligence, human valor, or divine order over the wild forces of nature.

The cultural and aesthetic manifestations of ancient Greece had a considerable space for these monstrosities and hybrids as well. They were commonly featured in vase paintings, sculptures, and architectural components, such as the metopes that were located atop the Parthenon.

Their impact may be seen in art and literature from succeeding periods in Western culture, extending well beyond the ancient world. They are mentioned in Dante's "Divine Comedy," as well as in Shakespeare's plays, and more recently, in the "Harry Potter" series written by J.K. Rowling and the "Percy Jackson" series written by Rick Riordan.

Through the examination of these beasts, not only do we achieve a more profound comprehension of the mythology of ancient Greece, but we also obtain new insights into the common human experience. These ageless stories continue to enthrall, confound, and motivate us, which serves as a useful reminder of the power of storytelling as well as the everlasting appeal of the mythical realm.

Chapter 6: The Underworld and Afterlife

The Realm of Hades

The ancient Greeks believed that after death, one entered the underworld, which was ruled over by their deity Hades. Within its murky domain down below, this dark plane was home to a wide variety of living and dead individuals from different time periods.

The Asphodel Meadows were home to ghostly figures that lacked either happiness or sadness. Nearby was a vast area known as the Elysian Fields, which offered anointed souls like Helen and Achilles the opportunity to enjoy eternal pleasure. When not presiding over the judgment halls of the Underworld, Hades and his spouse Persephone would make their home within the palace that belonged to Hades. Their three-headed guard dog, Cerberus, kept constant watch over the premises.

Both Tantalus, who was condemned to an eternity of thirst, and Sisyphus, who was condemned to an eternity of pushing his boulder up an infinite slope, were tormented as well. Some of the Eumenides assisted Hades in exacting punishment on those who broke their oaths or were disloyal. Elsewhere, recognizable shadows wandered free, each one clinging to a facet of their former existence but existing only as a phantom today.

There were also visits by mortals, such as Odysseus having conversations with shadows and Orpheus brazenly rescuing Eurydice from the underworld with the help of music. However, any vestiges that returned aboveground were met with the prospect of dissolving once more as shadows, their brief second life vanishing back into the everlasting night.

This realm reflected the Greeks' attempt to reconcile the fleeting nature of existence with their belief that vital essences or living memories would somehow endure for eternity inside the porous borders that exist between mortal and immortal, seen and unseen spheres of being. Their Underworld, despite being gruesome, was a place of meditation on the intertwining of existences amid the portals of death, which provided glimpses into secrets that were always beyond comprehension but always beckoned thinking minds.

Additional information on Hades and the Greek underworld are as follows:

The country of the dead was either encircled by rivers like the Acheron, Styx, Lethe, Phlegethon, and Cocytus, or it was traversed by these rivers.

Minos, Rhadamanthus, and Aeacus were the three judges who chose where each soul would spend its afterlife: Elysium, Asphodel Meadows, or Tartarus.

Tartarus, which was designated for those who rebelled against the gods like the Titans, was located deep below even the Asphodel Fields. It included fire pools and Stefan as well.

Despite lacking material, ghosts were able to keep their memories and personalities. They had to be appeased by libations in order to prevent them from causing damage to the living.

Rich individuals were occasionally laid to rest with monies inserted in their mouths so that boatman Charon might be paid for transporting them across the river Styx.

Cerberus, a gigantic dog with three heads, was stationed at the gate, along with other terrible beings such as gorgons.

In his job as the conductor of souls, Hermes Psychopomps frequently accompanied souls on their journeys to and from the world of the dead.

Constantly writhing and howling Torture was used as a form of punishment for lawbreakers, murderers, and oath-sworn individuals.

In Greek mythology, there were a few important methods that it was thought that spirits may transcend the rivers of the Underworld. These included the following:

- Charon, the ferryman: Charon would transport freshly arrived souls over the rivers Acheron or Styx onboard his boat, but only if they had money put on or in their lips as payment. Charon was known as the "ferryman of the underworld."

- Hermes Psychopomps: The guide of souls, Hermes would occasionally lead or transport souls to and from judgment before putting them into Charon's care. Hermes is also known as the psychopomp's.

- Consuming from Lethe: Prior to reincarnation or visiting the fields of Asphodel or Elysium, souls were required to consume from the River Lethe, which caused them to forget their previous life and prepare them for the next one.

- Crossing on stones or twigs: Some stories describe spirits across rivers by clinging onto pebbles or twigs that gave perilous floating. - Crossing on stones or twigs: Some myths describe souls traversing rivers by holding onto stones or twigs.

- Swimming or wading: If a soul was penniless and did not have any coin to pay Charon, the soul was forced to swim or wade through the dangerous aquatic obstacles on their own.

Therefore, the rivers presented a challenging last test, but it was believed that guides and vessels could assist the majority of souls in making their way into their new afterlife Domains inside Hades' realm. As a result, the Greeks believed that the Underworld was both mysterious and unavoidable. This led to the development of burial ceremonies and grave gifts intended to ease the passage of spirits.

The Rivers and Regions of the Greek Underworld

The Greek underworld, also known as the kingdom of the dead and controlled by Hades, is described as having a complex topography with many different areas and rivers. This gloomy world, which is inaccessible to living beings with the exception of a select number of heroes and demigods, is a fundamental component of Greek mythology and reflects ancient ideas of death and the afterlife.

The Five Rivers

It is stated that the Underworld is traversed by five rivers, each of which has its own unique significance.

1. Styx, also called the River of Hatred, was the most significant river in the Underworld. Styx was also known as the River of Hate. The gods

used it to make legally binding oaths, and when Achilles was a newborn, he was given a bath in it so that he would be immune to harm.

2. Acheron: Also known as the River of Pain or Sorrow, Acheron was the river that Charon, the ferryman, used to convey the souls of the deceased across.

3. Lethe, also known as the River of Forgetfulness, was a place where spirits went to drink in order to forget their life on earth. This amnesia was essential for the souls in order for them to be reborn.

4. Phlegethon, also called the River of Fire, was a stream of fire that went to Tartarus. It was also known by its Greek name, Phlegethon. It was a symbol of both devastation and cleansing.

5. The River of Wailing, also known as Cocytus, was known for its association with the act of weeping. It was thought to be the place where spirits went who had been mistreated or had not been buried.

The several realms that make up the underworld

The Underworld was split up into several different sections, each of which was reserved for a different kind of deceased person.

1. "Elysium": The Elysian Fields were a place that was only accessible to good people and heroic persons. It was a realm of unending joy and tranquility, very much like how we imagine Heaven to be in the present era.

2. "Asphodel Meadows" was the place in the afterlife where regular people would spend their time. It was a place with neither positive or negative connotations, serving neither as a reward nor a punishment.

3. "Tartarus" was the name of the region in the Underworld that was the most remote and was where the Titans were held captive. In addition to that, it was a realm of torment for the souls of those who had done evil. Mortals like as Sisyphus, Tantalus, and Ixion were among those who were condemned to suffer here for all eternity.

4. "The Mourning Fields": This area was set aside for people who had passed away as a result of their love for another person or an

unrequited love. It was a metaphor for the heartbreak that comes from love in this human life.

The Judges of the Dead

In addition to its topography, the Underworld was home to a number of characters who were responsible for passing judgment on the afterlives of the deceased. Based on the deeds performed by the person during their time on earth, three judges named Aeacus, Minos, and Rhadamanthus decided where the soul of each deceased person would spend eternity.

Taking on the Part of Hades

This region was governed by Hades, the god of the underworld, who was known for his strict justice. Hades was not a terrible character in ancient times, unlike what subsequent representations of Satan in Christianity have led many to believe. He was a dictator who was harsh but fair, and he made sure that the everlasting rules of death were adhered to.

Cerberus is known as the Watchdog of the Underworld.

The gateway to the underworld was guarded by Cerberus, the three-headed dog, who prevented the living from entering while also preventing the dead from departing. One of Heracles' Twelve Labors was to capture Cerberus, which the hero did without killing the beast out of respect for the Underworld and its inhabitants. Heracles was able to complete this labor successfully because he respected the Underworld.

The entrances to the underworld are called "The Gates."

On Earth, several passageways led down into the Underworld. One of the most well-known was at Acheron in Epirus, and it was thought that Charon would transport souls back and forth there. Necromancy, often known as talking to the dead, was a popular activity that people engaged in when visiting these locations.

The Fields of Punishment

Those souls who had committed transgressions against the gods would be punished here in this land of pain. Tantalus, who was constantly tormented by hunger and thirst but could never reach the food and drink that was nearby, and Sisyphus, who was doomed to push a rock upward only to have it roll back down again, are two famous inmates of Tantalus. Sisyphus was forced to roll the boulder uphill forever only to have it roll back down again.

Impact on the Development of Contemporary Culture

The Greek Underworld has exerted a significant influence on contemporary culture, penetrating not just literature and movies but also film and video games. For instance, in Dante's "Inferno," the organization of Hell is comparable to that of the Greek Underworld, with varying torments corresponding to the many crimes committed by the damned. The Underworld plays an important role in both the "Percy Jackson" series written by Rick Riordan and the "Hades" computer game that is so popular.

The ancient Greeks were interested in exploring life's moral and philosophical concerns, and their representation of the Greek Underworld reflects that interest. It emphasizes the significance of virtue, the reality that death is unavoidable, and the hope that there is justice in the afterlife. We not only dig into the rich tapestry of Greek mythology as we continue our research of these worlds and their occupants, but we also go on a deeper exploration of life, death, and what it means to be human as we make our way further into these realms. The Underworld, despite the gloomy atmosphere it exudes, is a rich source of information on the culture of ancient Greece, and it never ceases to enthrall us with the secrets it conceals. The Greek Underworld, with all of its varied areas and rivers, is a complex representation of the ancient Greeks' ideas of death and the proper conduct of one's afterlife. It functioned as a moral compass by making the promise of reward for those who were good and punishment for those who were evil. In addition, it brought solace and finality to the situation by suggesting that life will go on after death, albeit in a different form than before.

The idea of the Underworld and the different aspects that make up this notion have had a tremendous impact on subsequent civilizations and faiths. It is found in Roman mythology, where it has been adapted to fit its new setting, and it has had an impact on how Christians think about hell. Even in modern times, references to the Underworld and its inhabitants may be found in a wide variety of media, like as literature, films, and video games; this is a clear indication of the continuing power and allure of this setting.

It's interesting to note that the Underworld is more than simply a realm of fear and lamentation. It also offers comfort and a sense of completion, as well as the promise of continued presence after death, albeit in a different form than before. And even though the majority of the Underworld appears to be depressing and hopeless, there are some bright spots to be found there as well. The Elysian Fields provide a more upbeat perspective on the afterlife, acting as a ray of light amid an otherwise gloomy existence. The Greek concept of life and death was that they were two sides of the same coin, and neither could exist without the other. This duality between the dark and bright parts of the Underworld represents this concept.

The Dead, Punishments, and the Judgment of Souls

The Underworld is not just the domain of the dead in Greek mythology; rather, it is a sophisticated system in which the souls of the deceased are judged and either get their rightful reward or are punished according to their actions in life. This not only offers a foundation for morality by encouraging virtues and discouraging vices, but it also represents how ancient Greeks thought about life, death, and justice.

"The Journey of the Dead"

When a person dies, their spirit leaves their body and begins its trip to the afterlife, also known as the underworld. After being led there by Hermes, the psychopomps, also known as the "soul guide," the soul finally reaches the banks of the river Acheron. Here, the ferryman Charon takes the souls over the river, but only if they pay their price in the form of an obol, which is a currency that is put in the mouth of the departed prior to burial.

"The Judgment of Souls"

When the spirits reach the Underworld, they are subjected to judgment. Aeacus, Minos, and Rhadamanthus are the three judges who deliberate on the actions that a soul carried out during their time as a mortal. Rhadamanthus is in charge of judging the Western souls, while Aeacus is in charge of judging the Eastern souls. Minos casts the decisive vote.

The Asphodel Fields

The Asphodel Meadows are where the souls of the bulk of people, those who led lives that were neither exceptionally good nor bad, ended to after passing away. It was a wide plain that was covered in darkness, and the souls who resided there dwelt in a condition of oblivion, like shadows of their former selves.

Elysium and the Isles of the Blessed

Elysium is a realm of perpetual pleasure, tranquility, and beauty where the souls of the righteous, heroes, and those who were especially favored by the gods are said to have been sent. Some tales talk of a place called the Isles of the Blessed, which is described as an eternal paradise where those who chose to have multiple lives and worked their way up to Elysium end up to spend eternally.

The sign of Tara

The evil spirits were doomed to spend eternity in Tartarus, a dark and dreary abyss that lies beneath the Underworld. In this place, they were subjected to divine penalties that were appropriate to their deeds. Tantalus, who was sentenced to spend eternity unable to slake his thirst or satisfy his hunger as a result for killing his son; and Sisyphus, who was condemned to spend eternity rolling a rock up a hill, only to have it roll back down as a consequence for his dishonest nature. Both of these legendary people are said to have resided in Tartarus.

The practice of reincarnation

Reincarnation, also known as metempsychosis, was a concept that was popular among the ancient Greeks. Following a length of time spent in the Underworld as a metaphor, the souls would drink from the river Lethe, also known as the river of forgetfulness, and then make their way back up to the realm of the living in a new body so that they might start their lives over.

The Consequences of Eternity

The penalties that were meted out in Tartarus were, for the most part, tailored to the offenses that were committed. These penalties for all eternity were frequently humorous, as a reflection of the character of the individual's wrongdoings committed while they were still mortal. Tantalus, who was always being teased by food and wine that was just out of his reach, is a strong image of ravenous hunger as well as the futility of desire. In a same vein, Sisyphus, who was doomed to spend eternity performing meaningless labor, is symbolic of the pointlessness of deceit and treachery.

The Fields of Punishment

Those souls who had committed transgressions against the gods would be punished here in this land of pain. It was a desolate and scorching plain where the damned were punished with a variety of types of torment that would last forever. The ancient Greeks had the concept that the gods were righteous and that those who committed evil would, in the end, suffer divine vengeance. This belief served to promote societal standards and ethical conduct among the ancient Greeks.

The Function Played by the Furies

The Furies, also known as the Erinyes, were terrifying deities associated with retribution. They hunted out evildoers both on Earth and in the Underworld, driving them insane and causing them agony in the process. Their dogged pursuit of justice drives home the point that it is critically important to preserve society and familial links and that there are serious repercussions associated with breaching these sacred ties.

The Importance of a Decent Funeral and Burial

The ancient Greeks had the belief that if a person died without receiving a proper burial, their spirit would be unable to reach the Underworld and would instead be doomed to a life as a restless and unhappy ghost wandering the earth. This idea emphasizes the significance of rituals and societal obligations in Greek culture, and it plays a key role in a number of myths and tragedies, such as the narrative of Antigone, who disobeys the instructions of the king to ensure that her brother is buried in the correct manner.

Had an Effect on Subsequent Beliefs

The Greek Underworld, with its richly descriptive landscapes and moral judgements, has had a considerable impact on the subsequent development of faiths and ideologies. For example, the concepts of

Heaven and Hell found in Christianity share similarities with the concepts of Elysium and Tartarus. The concept of divine punishment and reward is also discussed at length in a great number of moral and intellectual debates all over the world.

The complex symbolism of the Greek Underworld offers some intriguing insights into the core values and beliefs held by ancient Greek civilization. It was believed that those who committed immoral acts would spend their eternity in the dull Fields of Asphodel or the terrible depths of Tartarus, both of which functioned as effective deterrents. At the same time, the incentive of the promise of perpetual pleasure in Elysium or the Isles of the Blessed motivated heroic behavior and virtuous behavior.

In general, these stories present a nuanced and intricate interpretation of life, death, and morality. They give the impression that the choices we make in this world have repercussions that last for all of eternity. In spite of the fact that they come from a long time ago, these stories nevertheless have a powerful impact on us today, prompting us to consider the mysteries of life, death, and what is beyond. The ethical and moral standards of ancient Greek civilization are reflected in the beliefs that ancient Greeks had towards death, judgment, and the afterlife. They encouraged admirable qualities such as devotion, bravery, and intelligence, while discouraging less admirable traits such as hubris, dishonesty, and disdain for both fellow humans and the gods.

In addition, by studying these tales, one might have a better understanding of the ancient Greek perspective on life and death. They viewed life as an opportunity to pursue perfection and morality, and death as the inevitable end that brought judgment and a reasonable recompense or punishment, depending on how one lived their life.

These views have had a tremendous impact on the development of philosophy, literature, and art in Western culture. The writings of philosophers such as Pythagoras and Plato, as well as epic poetry such as the Iliad and the Odyssey and plays written by Sophocles and Euripides, contain examples of these. It is a tribute to their ongoing popularity and significance that they continue to inspire current interpretations and adaptations in many mediums such as novels, movies, and video games.
The meaning of life, the nature of death, the possibility of an afterlife, and the idea of justice are only some of the topics that are brought up

in discussion by these myths, and their importance extends well beyond that of their historical and cultural significance. They encourage us to give these ageless issues more thought, which in turn deepens our comprehension of both ourselves and the world around us.

Chapter 7: Archaeological Sites and Artifacts

Temples, Sanctuaries, and Other Sacred Sites

In ancient Greek civilization, temples and sanctuaries played an essential role in the religious life of the people. These holy places played an essential role in the day-to-day activities, ceremonies, and the construction of the identities of the city-states.

The landscape was dominated by massive temples, like as the Parthenon in Athens, whose beautiful construction amplified the grandeur of the resident gods. Even smaller temples were home to key deities, ranging from Zeus to patrons of the community. The oracle of Delphi was said to have spoken from amongst serpents near the purported navel of the earth. Other natural places had significance as well. The groves provided a safe haven, whilst the grottoes surrounding the springs encouraged assembly.

The holy precincts were used, although worship also took place outside in the open air. The animals that were sacrificed and the sacrifices were brought to the altars. The coastal promontories and cairns served as a navigational aid for mariners, and their guardian statues could be seen from a great distance. Even the mythical portals to Hades had temples for appeasing the chthonic forces that resided there.

However, spirituality existed outside the confines of physical architecture. In homes, around ancestral hearths, and on battlefields that enshrined heroism, religion penetrated everyday life. Regardless of location, communities are spiritually connected together by the performance of communal civic responsibilities such as plays, songs, and processions.

The Greeks believed that the framework of life was established not by seclusion in temples but by their beliefs. More so than via building alone, they found their connection to the divine through the natural world, rituals, and shared experiences. Despite the fact that architectural ruins have been preserved, the living heritage represents religion's wellsprings pouring beyond any buildings and into the fundamental foundations of civilization. Ancient Greeks intertwined their religious practices with all elements of life, including politics and

their sense of identity. This is reflected in the sacred places they created.
Information on holy locations in ancient Greece:

- Sanctuaries, also known as temenos, are sacred wooded places that were used to house worshippers, as well as to hold ceremonies, festivals, and athletic competitions.

- Hera are locations that venerate deified mortal heroes by having altars and occasionally tomb-monuments on the grounds. Served as places for religious pilgrimage.

- Prophets would visit significant oracular sites like as Delphi, Dodona, and Troponins' cave in order to seek guidance from the oracles there.

- Groves were places of worship, and they frequently included temples and altars. For example, the oak grove at Dodona was the location of Zeus' oracle.

- Mountains: Summits were associated with the divine and served as sites for ritual sacrifices, just as Greece's Holy Mountain Olympus, which was ruled over by the gods.

- Lakes: Bodies of water, like as the holy lakes linked with places in Epirus and Boeotia, lured worshipers to their shores.

- Caves: Distant caverns, such as the Prytanea caves, served as gateways to the underworld and locations of prophesy. Among these caves are the Prytanea caves.

- Boundary stones: Sacred monuments that served as altars at crossroads and marked territory under the protection of Hermes.

The Oracle and Sanctuary of Delphi in Ancient Greece was Without a Doubt the Most Significant Sacred Site in All of Ancient Greece. The following are some of the primary reasons that it was regarded as being so crucial:

- The legendary Pythia oracle of Apollo was located here, and its predictions were used to inform important political choices and colonization efforts throughout the Greek world.

- Location of the renowned omphalos stone, which was said to have marked the exact geographical center of the world. Because of this, its authority and status increased.
- Due to the fact that it was governed by affluent monks who, over the course of ages, accumulated treasures, Delphi became an extremely wealthy and politically significant city.

- Was the site of the illustrious Pythian Games, one of the four Panhellenic festivals that contributed to the cultural unification of the Greeks.

- Ruled as a neutral sanctuary that even city-states who were at war with each other respected, which enabled it to mediate peace deals.

Delphi was the most revered location for the worship of Apollo, which was one of the most well-known and well-respected deities in Greek religion. Delphi was the most significant location in terms of religion, prophesy, and Hellenic cultural identity across the Greek world for many centuries. This is despite the fact that other locations, such as Olympia and Athens, also had a great deal of significance.

Therefore, the Greeks erected locations in both nature and architecture that connected their communities, rituals, and national mythologies inextricably to god. These sites were found in both natural and man-made environments.

Treasures and Artifacts Found at Key Locations

The stories of the heroes of Greek mythology are frequently endowed with mythical jewels and artifacts, which are either bestowed upon them by the gods or found in distant regions. These things, which were endowed with magical qualities, played significant parts in a variety of tales and served as symbols of divine favor, heroism, or the search of knowledge.

The Fleece of Gold

One of the most renowned artifacts in Greek mythology is called the Golden Fleece, and it is described as the golden fleece that came from a mythical ram. The achievement of this goal, which represented royalty and authority, was the purpose of Jason's journey. The Golden

Fleece was stored at Colchis, under the watchful eye of a dragon that never stopped breathing, until Jason, with the assistance of Princess Medea, was able to take it.

Hermes.

The person who wore the sandals with wings associated with Hermes, the messenger of the gods, had the power to fly. Perseus was on a mission to slay Medusa, and Hermes helped him out by lending him his sandals. Hermes, the Greek deity of travelers and frontiers, is connected with the qualities of swiftness and independence, which are represented by the sandals.

Helm of Darkness

The Helm of Darkness, which was also referred to as the Cap of Invisibility, was a potent relic that turned whoever wore it into an invisible being. Although it was most commonly linked to Hades, the deity of the underworld, Athena and Hermes were also known to make use of the symbol. In his efforts to defeat Medusa, Perseus made use of it.

The word "Aegis"

The Aegis was a heavenly shield that typically displayed the severed head of Medusa. It was commonly linked with the goddess Athena. It was a representation of heavenly might and protection. Heroes, like as Heracles and Perseus, were frequently allowed to borrow the Aegis from Athena.

The Box of Pandora

In the ancient Greek stories, Pandora's Box was really a jar, and it housed all of the evils that were in the earth. Because of her curiosity, Pandora, the first woman, opened the box, and by doing so, she let all of these horrors out into the world. When she shut it once again, Hope was the only one who stayed inside. The fable of Pandora's Box is a cautionary story that teaches listeners a lesson about the dangers of insatiable curiosity and disobedience.

The source of contention

Eris, the goddess of discord, is said to have brought the "Apple of Discord," a golden apple engraved with the inscription "to the fairest," to a feast that was held by the gods. This apple, which was fought over by Hera, Athena, and Aphrodite, was eventually the cause of the Trojan War. This goes to demonstrate how something that appears to be completely innocuous can really result in a great deal of conflict.

The Bow of Artemis

Artemis, the Greek goddess of the hunt, was shown as using a silver bow, which was a representation of both her dominance over nature and her function as a huntress. Because Artemis was considered to be a virgin goddess, the bow, which was frequently connected with the moon, was also considered to be a sign of chastity and purity.

The trident of Poseidon

The mighty trident that was wielded by Poseidon, the god of the sea, was a potent representation of his authority over the waterways. Poseidon has the power to generate springs, still the waves, and trigger earthquakes with it. There are three prongs on a trident, and they have been understood as representing the three different states that the sea might be in: calm, fluctuating, and stormy.

The Caduceus

As the messenger of the gods, Hermes was represented by the Caduceus, which consisted of a staff that was twisted by two serpents and capped with wings. It was an emblem of both peace and trade since Hermes was known for his role as a peacemaker and a defender of businesspeople. In modern times, the Caduceus has come to be identified with the field of medicine; however, the actual emblem for medicine is the Rod of Asclepius, which consists of a single serpent and does not have wings.

The lightning bolts that Zeus

The thunderbolts that Zeus wielded were both his primary weapon and a symbol of his power. The lightning bolts were emblematic of Zeus' position as the god of the sky and of his authority over the elements, and they were fashioned by the Cyclops. Those who disobeyed divine law or did terrible deeds may be punished with these implements of punishment. They were employed to execute justice.

The lyre that belonged to Apollo

Apollo, the Greek deity of music and poetry, was often shown playing a lyre, which is a stringed musical instrument. Hermes, according to the legend, was the one who came up with the idea and then offered it to Apollo as a gesture of goodwill. Apollo, the god of arts and order, is associated with the lyre, which is symbolic of harmony, creativity, and civilization.

These legendary items and jewels, with their deep connotations and pivotal roles in the myths that surround them, provide intriguing insights into the ancient Greek worldview. They highlight the abilities and territories of the gods, the values and goals of the civilization, and the moral precepts that are ingrained in the tales.

These artifacts have influenced various facets of society and knowledge in addition to the mythology in which they play a significant role. They have been the impetus for works of art, literature, and music, and they have also made their way into the lexicon of science and the symbolism of modern times. Despite its historical connections to business and bargaining, the caduceus is now commonly recognized as a symbol of medicine and healthcare.

In addition to this, the fabled objects encourage us to think about the power and responsibility that come along with having exceptional skills and capabilities. They serve as a reminder that the qualities of knowledge, bravery, and justice that are represented by these holy riches are the genuine keys to overcoming obstacles and attaining our objectives. As we continue to investigate these objects and the meanings behind them, not only do we find out more about the intricate web of Greek mythology, but we also find out ageless truths about human nature and the human experience. Treasures and relics like this aren't only there to further the story; they also hold a tremendous amount of symbolic weight. They frequently serve as metaphors for the characteristics of the gods who hold or bestow them, the virtues or vices of the heroes who pursue them, and the ethical teachings that myths attempt to impart to their audiences.

In addition to this, the cultural manifestations that have been affected by these relics include anything from movies and video games to literature and visual art. They continue to pique people's interest, which results in the creation of new works of fiction and adaptations. Our knowledge of this fascinating culture and its long mythology is enhanced by the riches and artifacts that were discovered in ancient Greece. These objects provide us with new perspectives on the ancient Greeks' beliefs, morals, and methods of storytelling.

In addition, the searches for these relics are frequently used as opportunities for the protagonists to demonstrate their value, face their fears, or address their weaknesses. These excursions include not only the heroes' bodies but also their minds and spirits, serving as a metaphor for the heroes' maturation and development as they go through the missions. In this regard, these artifacts and the journeys to acquire them are reflections of the human experience, complete with all of its tribulations, transformations, and victories.

Ancient Texts and Manuscripts Related to the Myths

The oldest accounts of Greek mythology were passed down orally over the course of millennia before they were committed to writing. Poetic works by Homer, such as the Iliad and Odyssey, are credited with laying the groundwork for later depictions of the aftermath of the Trojan War. Hesiod's Theogony and Works and Days both contain educational stories in which the gods are given specific duties to play in the development of the universe.

Literacy led to the systematic codification of myths during the peak of classical civilization. Diodorus was responsible for the cataloguing of Roman artifacts that were housed at the Library of History. Throughout his description of Greece, Pausanias collected documentation on many locations, places, and oral traditions. Within Bibliotheca, Apollodorus came to represent the heroic deeds and trees of the Olympians. In his work "Metamorphoses," Ovid reimagined ancient myths and stories from a Roman perspective.

However, transmission was dependent on the talents of solitary storytellers who passed down memories around hearths for decades on their own. Only fragments of scrolls and manuscripts like Athenaeus' academic dinners managed to escape the fire that swept across

Alexandria. Myths, however, persisted among the mosaics and ceramics that decorated daily Roman life because each generation recounted the stories of their ancestors.

The classical education that we still possess now was carefully preserved by monks in the middle ages who painstakingly copied books by hand. Their conscientious work as scribes assured that mythology would survive well beyond any age. Myths continue to serve as history's shared wellspring, giving metaphors that represent the human condition throughout all periods. These myths are now collected digitally. Their legacy is not only in the words that have been written, but also in the spirits that live within each of us.

The advent of new technology brings with it some dangers, but the digitization of old manuscripts paves the way for wider access to a variety of viewpoints that span both place and time. The awareness of our shared roots and our sense of camaraderie are both strengthened by the sharing of stories. May records from the past as well as the present continue to enlighten searchers with the timeless truths contained in mythology.

Information on older books and manuscripts related to Greek mythology, including:

- Linear B tablets are the earliest writings that are known to exist. They date back to around 1200 BCE and contain lists of gods, sacrifices, and tales on tablets written in Aegean script.

- Classical writings include works written on papyrus scrolls by authors such as Homer, Hesiod, Sappho, Aeschylus, Sophocles, and Euripides. These scrolls were discovered at archaeological sites like as Oxyrhynchus.

- Scholia is a term that refers to the marginal notes and commentary on classical texts that were written by scribes during the Byzantine era. These annotations and commentary attempted to debunk many falsehoods.

- Lexicons are reference works that summarize stories, deities, and characters. Examples of such texts include the Suda, which gathered hundreds of years' worth of scholarly work.

- Travel guides: Works such as Pausanias' Description of Greece documented regional variances and local worship practices in Greece.

- Bestiaries: These collections were written in the late ancient period, and they detailed mythological monsters through mosaic depictions and vase paintings.

- The preservation of legendary lore through the use of manuscript traditions: monastic copying of books in medieval Greek, Latin, and vernacular languages.

- Mythographic summaries: Late works presented myths in the shape of an encyclopedia for the purposes of teaching and reference.

Therefore, myths were transmitted through a variety of written forms, which recorded Greek myth-telling over a wide range of eras and geographical locations.

Chapter 8: The Legacy and Influence of Greek Myths

Myths in Later Greek and Roman Times

In subsequent eras, particularly during the Hellenistic period (323-31 BC) and Roman times (753 BC-476 AD), Greek mythology suffered substantial changes. As the cultural, political, and philosophical landscapes of a society changed, new interpretations evolved, new gods were created, and myths were modified to accommodate these shifts.

Transformations During the Hellenistic Period
Following Alexander the Great's conquests and throughout the time known as the Hellenistic period, Greek culture and mythology began to expand over the Eastern Mediterranean and into the Near East. This resulted in the blending of Greek mythology with the traditions of the area, which gave rise to the creation of new gods and tales.

One such example is the cult of Serapis, a god who, in Egyptian mythology, combines characteristics of Osiris and Apis with components that come from Hellenistic religion. This time period is also distinguished by the proliferation of mystery cults, such as those dedicated to Dionysus and Orpheus. These cults featured initiation procedures that promised individual salvation and a happy afterlife, which reflected the trend of the time period toward more personalized religious experiences.

Roman modifications and adaptations
The Romans appropriated and adapted Greek mythology to their own pantheon through a process known as interpretation Romana when they came into touch with Greek culture. This technique is named after them. The similarity in characteristics and purposes of Greek and Roman gods led to their identification with one another. Zeus was then recognized as Jupiter, Hera was renamed Juno, Aphrodite was given the title of Venus, and so on.

Roman poets such as Virgil, Ovid, and Horace reinterpreted Greek tales, frequently including their own unique perspectives or concentrating on other elements of the stories. For example, Virgil's "Aeneid" places the

Trojan hero Aeneas at the heart of the tale, connecting the creation of Rome with the aftermath of the Trojan War. Aeneas is referred to as "the charioteer."

Approaches to Myth from a Philosophical Standpoint
The later Greek and Roman philosophers frequently interpreted tales using an allegorical framework. The Neoplatonists saw myths to be symbolic representations of philosophical truths, but the Stoics interpreted myths as allegories of actual facts.

For instance, the Roman poet Ovid does a retelling of Greek stories in his work "Metamorphoses," and he does it in a way that reflects philosophical and moral principles. In a similar manner, the philosopher Plato explained the concepts he was trying to convey via the use of myths, such as the tale of the cave and the myth of Er.

Continued Influence and Persistence in the Field
Myths continued to have significance and allure despite being retold and altered over time, yet these factors did not diminish them. They continued to be pervasive in art, literature, and everyday life, functioning as a cultural touchstone and common language. Myths were an essential component of Greek and Roman culture, and their influence can be seen everywhere from the splendor of the Parthenon in Athens to the paintings in Pompeii, as well as in the performances of tragedies in theaters and the tales recounted over the dinner table.

Mythology and the Propaganda of the Imperial State
Mythology was utilized by political leaders throughout the history of both the Hellenistic kingdoms and the Roman Empire. In order to legitimize their reign and further their goals, they aligned themselves with legendary figures, such as heroes and gods. For example, Alexander the Great said that his ancestry came from Heracles and Achilles, while Roman emperors frequently identified themselves as being sprung from Jupiter or Hercules.

Mythology and the Construction of Cultural Identities
Myths were a mechanism through which Greek and Roman societies were able to maintain their cultural identity and superiority when they interacted with other cultures. In spite of the fact that the Romans relied largely on Greek mythology as a source of inspiration, they modified the stories so that they reflected Roman beliefs and history,

so demonstrating the exceptionality and superiority of Roman civilization.

New Meanings for Old Myths
A great number of myths have been rethought or recounted with new accents or conclusions added to them. For instance, the Romans attributed their ancestry back to Troy, hence in certain Roman accounts of the Trojan War, the Trojans were shown in a more sympathetic light than in other versions. Aeneas, a hero from the Trojan War, was portrayed in Roman mythology as the archetypal Roman, exemplifying noble qualities such as piety and responsibility.

The Role of Mythology in Contemporary Culture
Myths continued to infiltrate all aspects of daily life, including cultural events and rites, artistic creations, and written works. They supplied tales and symbols that were commonly understood, which helped shape social norms and cultural values. In Hellenistic and Roman art, mythological subjects were frequently used for decoration, appearing on anything from monumental buildings to everyday objects.

The Study of Mythology and Religion
Mythology was deeply ingrained in both the Greek and Roman religious traditions. The origins of gods, rituals, and religious organizations were explained through the telling of myths. In addition to this, they provided moral and practical direction, explained natural occurrences, and offered solace in the face of the unpredictability of life.

The Greek Mythological Tradition and Its Enduring Legacy
The fundamental components of Greek mythology have not changed significantly over the course of their long history. Their ongoing appeal was secured by the presence of universal themes, interesting characters, and rich symbolism in their stories. They were a rich source of ideas that following generations of writers, artists, philosophers, and psychologists drew upon for their work.

The modern world is not immune to the enduring influence of Greek mythology. They may be found in a huge variety of situations, ranging from the names of planets to the ideas behind psychological theories. They act as metaphors in political and cultural debate, as well as serve as sources of inspiration for books, movies, and video games. They are utilized in the process of branding and marketing, such as in the case of the Nike and Amazon logos.

As we go deeper into the mythology of later Greek and Roman civilizations, we come across an intricate web of tales that mirror the many facets of the human experience. We may observe how myths develop alongside cultures, shifting to accommodate new circumstances and requirements but still preserving their essential nature. These myths, which serve as reflections of the human experience and carriers of ageless knowledge, continue to captivate, motivate, and direct us in our lives. They serve as a constant reminder of our connected humanity, our ongoing adversities, and the heroism that lies latent inside each of us. The adaptions and reimagining of Greek tales that occurred during subsequent periods of Greek and Roman history are evidence of the myths' ongoing popularity and adaptability. They are a reflection of the ways in which civilizations absorb, reinterpret, and reuse components from one another, of the ways in which beliefs and narratives vary through time, and of the ways in which myths may be overlaid with new meanings while yet keeping their essential essence.

These reinterpretations of Greek mythology have continued to have an impact on modern Western ideas, as well as Western literature and art. They have been the catalyst for the creation of works of art such as Dante's "Divine Comedy," Shakespeare's plays, and even contemporary works such as Rick Riordan's "Percy Jackson" series. As we explore further into these later tales and their adaptations, not only do we increase our understanding of the Greek and Roman civilizations, but we also acquire insights into the eternal and global attraction that mythology possesses.

Representations in Art and Literature Over the Centuries

Throughout the years, Greek mythology has been a significant inspiration for works of art and literature. Its engrossing storytelling, deep symbolism, and multifaceted characters have served as the impetus for a vast array of artistic endeavors, ranging from Renaissance paintings and ceramics to contemporary books and films. The profundity and pervasiveness of these beliefs are demonstrated by the myths' continuing appeal.

Representations from Antiquity
Myths were represented in a variety of different types of art throughout ancient Greece. Mythological depictions, like as Heracles' labors or the Trojan War, were frequently used as subject matter for paintings on vases. Temples were decked up with statues and friezes that portrayed gods and heroes in various guises. Because of these graphic representations, myths were made available to individuals of varying reading levels.

Reinterpretations of works from the Middle Ages and the Renaissance
During the Middle Ages, many Greek myths were transformed into Christian allegories so that they could be used in Christian tales. Allegorical interpretations were widespread among medieval intellectuals. One example of this would be the view of Hercules as a metaphor of Christ's triumph over sin.

The study of Greek mythology had a renaissance during the time period of the Renaissance. Myths were a source of inspiration for many artists, including Botticelli, Michelangelo, and Titian, who used them to investigate topics like love, power, and beauty. For example, in "The Birth of Venus" by Botticelli, the goddess Venus is seen emerging from the water to represent beauty and love.

Adaptations in the Romantic and Victorian Styles
During the Romantic period, poets such as Keats and Byron turned to mythology as a means to explore the sublime and communicate their profound feelings. While Keats' "Ode on a Grecian Urn" ruminates on an image from a Greek vase, Byron's "Prometheus" portrays the Titan as a symbol of stubborn independence through the lens of the character Prometheus.

Authors of the Victorian era were likewise interested in Greek myths. For instance, the hero Odysseus from Tennyson's "Ulysses" is reimagined as an elderly monarch who is longing for one last adventure.

Applications in the Modern and Contemporary Era
Novels, plays, and movies written and produced in the 20th and 21st centuries have breathed fresh life into Greek tales. Myths have been rewritten by authors such as James Joyce and Margaret Atwood in order to examine contemporary topics. While "Ulysses" by James Joyce draws parallels between the travels of Odysseus and a day in the life of a

modern Dubliner, "The Penelope" by Margaret Atwood retells the story of the Odyssey from Penelope's point of view.

Greek mythology have also been an inspiration for works of fantasy fiction, such as the "Harry Potter" and "Percy Jackson" series written by J.K. Rowling and Rick Riordan, respectively.

The Representation of Greek Mythology in Visual Art and Film

Greek mythology continue to serve as a source of creativity for the visual arts, including painting, sculpture, graphic design, and fashion. They have also been made into a large number of movies and television programs, including "Clash of the Titans," "Troy," and "Hercules."

The Tragedies and Comedies of Ancient Greece

Mythology was a significant component in the development of ancient Greek theater. Mythological tales were frequently retold in dramatic form in tragedies in order to examine topics like fate, hubris, and divine justice. Myth provides a substantial foundation for dramatic works such as "Oedipus Rex" by Sophocles and "Medea" by Euripides. Even comedies made references to mythology and would occasionally make fun of heroic tales or gods.

Art in the Neoclassical Style
The mythology of ancient Greece, in particular, saw a renaissance of interest throughout the Neoclassical period. Mythological subjects were frequently employed by artists such as Jacques-Louis David to communicate ethical and political ideas to their audiences. The Roman fable "The Intervention of the Sabine Women" is shown in his picture, and the message it conveys is one of advocacy for peace.

The Movements of Symbolism and Surrealism
Greek mythology has had an influence on a number of modern art groups. Painters who adhered to the symbolist movement expressed abstract thoughts and feelings via the use of mythical symbols. Artists of the surrealist movement, such as Salvador Dal, explored the subconscious mind by incorporating mythical motifs into dreamy settings in their work.

The Relationship Between Psychoanalysis and Myth
The field of psychology, particularly psychoanalysis, has been significantly influenced by Greek mythology. Both Sigmund Freud and Carl Jung looked to mythology for inspiration and explanation while developing their psychological theories. For example, the Oedipus complex refers to a child's thoughts of yearning for the parent of the opposite sex as well as feelings of competition with the parent of the same sex. This complex was named after the fabled king Oedipus.

Literary Analysis and Philosophical Concepts
Even literary theory and criticism have been shaped by mythology at some point. In his work "Anatomy of Criticism," Northrop Frye presents a theory of myths and archetypes in writing, which draws extensively on Greek mythology as a source of inspiration. Theorists that adhere to the structuralist and poststructuralist schools of thought have investigated myths as systems of signification, focusing on the myths' fundamental components and the cultural roles they play.

Fictions of Science and the Fantastic
The ancient Greek myths have been reinterpreted and given new life in many works of science fiction and fantasy literature. They give writers with generic storylines, characters, and ideas that may be adapted to fit a variety of speculative contexts. The books "Ilium" and "Olympos" by Dan Simmons, for instance, retell the story of the Trojan War set in the future on Mars.

Graphic novels as well as comic books
The ancient Greek tales have been brought to the attention of modern readers thanks to graphic novel and comic book adaptations. For example, George O'Connor's "Olympians" series retells the mythology of the gods in a fashion that is lively and aesthetically fascinating. These books focus on the gods of ancient Greece.

These examples demonstrate the enormous breadth and depth of the effect that Greek mythology has had on art and literature. They are evidence of the adaptability and vitality of these ancient legends, demonstrating their ability to inspire and resound across a variety of time periods, cultural contexts, and forms of expression.

The adaptability of myths is further demonstrated by these many versions. They are able to be rethought, reimagined, and recounted in an infinite number of ways, which makes them applicable to a wide variety of societies, time eras, and individuals. They encourage us to interact with them imaginatively, to come up with our own interpretations, and to carry on the time-honored practice of telling stories.

The ever-present impact that Greek myths have had on art and literature is another example that highlights the significance of mythology in human society. Myths are a link to our history, an enrichment to our present, and a source of inspiration for our future. They assist us in understanding the world around us, gaining insight into the intricacies of the human condition, and imagining new possibilities. As we continue to investigate and develop new interpretations of these age-old stories, we are taking part in the age-old human search for comprehension, expression, and connection.

Myths That Continue to Inspire Our Culture Today

The vast tapestry of gods, heroes, and monsters that is found in Greek mythology continues to have a significant impact on our society today. Its enduring concepts, riveting storytelling, and archetypal characters reverberate over time and space, finding manifestations in works of literature, art, psychology, and advertising, and even in scientific research and technological development.

Literature and the Moving Image
The Greek myths have had a significant impact on a variety of literary genres and forms, from traditional novels to contemporary fiction. Greek myths are retold by authors such as Madeline Miller in her award-winning books "The Song of Achilles" and "Circe," which each take a unique approach to the stories. Young readers are introduced to classic stories through the well-known "Percy Jackson" book series by Rick Riordan, which retells Greek mythology by placing its gods and heroes in modern-day settings.

Greek mythology is the source of inspiration for a broad variety of cinema genres, ranging from epic dramas like "Troy" and "Clash of the Titans" to animated movies like Disney's "Hercules." The myths are brought to life on the big screen by these adaptations, which captivate viewers with their ageless tales of valor, adventure, and metamorphosis.

The Worlds of Art and Architecture

Greek mythology continues to be an influential source for the visual arts, including but not limited to painting, sculpture, fashion design, and graphic design. Mythological stories, with all the rich symbolism they contain and the dramatic tension they generate, offer a limitless well of ideas for creative expression.

In the field of architecture, the influence of Greek mythology may be observed in structures designed in the style of classical Greece, as well as in the ornamental features of buildings. As an illustration, the Statue of Liberty, despite the fact that it is not an exact portrayal of a Greek goddess, symbolizes the spirit of Libertas, the Roman counterpart of the Greek goddess Eleuthera, which represents freedom.

The study of psychology

The ideas put out by Freud and Jung, in particular, may be seen to have been affected by Greek mythology. Both Freud's Oedipus complex and Jung's archetypes have significant roots in Greek mythology and make extensive use of these stories in order to investigate the complexity of the human mind. These fantastic stories continue to provide us with new perspectives on our dreams, anxieties, and wants, as well as the problems we face.

Advertising and brand building are both important.

Greek myths are frequently used in marketing and branding by businesses as a means of communicating the messages or ideals associated with their brands. For instance, the sports brand Nike, which was named after the Greek goddess of victory, used mythology to represent athletic success. In a similar vein, the Amazon logo, which has an arrow pointing from A to Z, is reminiscent of the ancient Greek story of the Aegis, Zeus's all-encompassing shield, and also suggests that the corporation provides a diverse selection of products.

The fields of Science and Technology

The influence of Greek mythology may be seen all the way through to science and technology. Numerous celestial entities, ranging from planets to asteroids, take their names from deities and heroes from Greek mythology. The name of a chemical element is derived from Tantalus, a mythological ruler who was condemned by the gods to an eternity of thirst and hunger.

The Performing Arts and Music

Many pieces of music and performances in the performing arts have been influenced by Greek mythology. These ageless tales are frequently the inspiration for operas, ballets, and musicals. For example, Richard Strauss' opera "Elektra" is a retelling of the Greek tragedy of Electra and her quest for vengeance against her mother, Clytemnestra. The story of Orpheus and Eurydice is given a contemporary spin in the musical "Hades town" that plays on Broadway.

The phrase "Video Games"
The stories and characters from Greek mythology are frequently included in video games. For example, the protagonist, Kratos, a Spartan warrior, is at the center of the "God of War" series. Kratos engages in dialogue with many gods, goddesses, and fantastical beasts. The famous video game "Hades" depicts the adventures of Zagreus, the son of Hades, as he tries to find a way out of the underworld. Players of these games are completely submersed in the expansive universe of Greek mythology, therefore exposing a new generation to these time-honored stories.

Industry of Fashion
The fashion industry is not immune to the impact of Greek mythology. Mythological stories and symbols are frequently used by designers as sources of inspiration for their collections. Gianni Versace picked the head of the Medusa for the Versace logo because he believed it embodied the qualities of power, strength, and beauty. The Versace logo is one of the most recognizable trademarks in the fashion industry.

The fields of Education and Philosophy
The study of literature, history, philosophy, psychology, and other academic disciplines all benefit greatly from the incorporation of Greek mythology. They are utilized in the classroom as teaching tools to explain ethical principles, investigate aspects of human nature, and encourage analytical thought. In addition to this, they offer a plentiful source for references in works of literature and art, which helps to improve cultural literacy.

Culture and the Media in the Public Eye
The popular culture and the media are saturated with Greek mythology. They provide authors of books, movies, and television shows with ideas for characters and stories. They are often used in common language and idioms, such as "Pandora's box" to refer to a source of unexpected troubles, "Achilles' heel" to refer to a weakness, and "Herculean task" to refer to a big project.

These examples demonstrate the continuing effect that Greek mythology has had as well as its flexibility. They illustrate how these ancient stories continue to reverberate with us now, providing a rich source of motivation, insight, and comprehension in the process. They serve as a reminder of the power that myths have to unite people across time and cultures, to shed light on the human condition, to excite our imaginations, and to make our lives more meaningful.

In a world that is becoming more interdependent and globalized, the Greek myths serve to remind us of our common humanity and the overarching themes that bind us together. They inspire us to consider our core beliefs, face our anxieties, and work toward achieving our goals by motivating us to do so. They encourage us to continue investigating, questioning, and creating in order to make a contribution to the age-old discussion about what it means to be human. These instances are illustrative of the broad effect that Greek mythology has had on our contemporary culture. These ancient stories, which have been passed down from generation to generation, continue to educate, inspire, and delight modern audiences. They excite our imagination by reflecting our most profound feelings, resonating with the human experiences that we all have had, and connecting us emotionally.

In addition, the Greek myths teach us the importance of having a good narrative to tell. They demonstrate how tales can cross the borders of culture and time, as well as connect us to our history and provide us with inspiration for the future. As we continue to investigate and reassess the meaning of these myths, we are taking part in an age-old practice of storytelling, which contributes to the growth of our cultural legacy as well as our comprehension of the human experience.

Made in the USA
Monee, IL
26 October 2023